MORE MODERN AMERICAN POETS

MORE MODERN AMERICAN POETS

By James G. Southworth

Essay Index Reprint Series

Essay Index

BOOKS FOR LIBRARIES PRESS
FREEPORT, NEW YORK

First Published 1954

Reprinted 1968 by arrangement
with Basil Blackwell and Mott, Ltd.

INTERNATIONAL STANDARD BOOK NUMBER:
0-8369-0889-9

LIBRARY OF CONGRESS CATALOG CARD NUMBER:
68-54371

PRINTED IN THE UNITED STATES OF AMERICA
BY
NEW WORLD BOOK MANUFACTURING CO., INC.
HALLANDALE, FLORIDA 33009

Table of Contents

Preface

THE present collection of essays, like those in *Some Modern American Poets* (1950), is intended for the general reader and not for the specialist. It is not so much a continuation as a rounding out both chronologically and from the point of view of tradition. It should add light and shade to the general impression given by the earlier volume. Listing the poets in the two volumes chronologically, with those of the present one starred, the relationship is clearer: Dickinson (1830-1886), Robinson (1869-1935), Frost (1875-   ), Stevens (1879-   ), Williams* (1883-   ), Pound* (1885-   ), Wylie* (1885-1928), Jeffers (1887-   ), Marianne Moore* (1887-   ), Ransom* (1888-   ), Aiken* (1889-   ), MacLeish (1892-   ), Van Doren* (1894-   ), Cummings (1894-   ), Hillyer* (1895-   ), Benèt (1898-1943), Tate* (1899-   ), Crane (1899-   ), Riding* (1901-   ), Robert Penn Warren* (1905-   ), Auden* (1907-   ). In the first volume the majority of the poets were content to work within the tradition; in the present one, eight of the twelve have attempted to alter and to re-invigorate that tradition from various sources.

Many readers will question the choice of poets for individual treatment. Although the choice is not entirely my own, the final responsibility, of course, rests with me. I have tried to learn from others which poets to include. It should be evident from my criticisms where the labour has been one of love or duty. Often what began as a labour of duty ended as a labour of love, and vice versa. But whether of love or duty, I have gained much from it, particularly a fresh orientation to the literature of the past.

The importance of this fresh orientation is difficult to over-stress. As Mr. Sigfried Giedion has pointed out in his *Space,*

Time and Architecture (1943) "the historian . . . must be in close contact with contemporary conceptions." This is not only true of the historian, but of the critic who would find in the literature of the past those qualities important for the present. Because, again to quote Mr. Giedion, "no generation is privileged to grasp a work of art from all sides; each *actively living* generation discovers new aspects of it." The italics are mine. The new aspects, however, will not be discovered by the critic unless he shows in the field of criticism the same courage and energy the artists have displayed in theirs. What is true for the critic is likewise true for the person interested in prosody.

I have learned, for example, too, the futility of attempting to use classical terminology as a means of indicating the prosodic patterns. Not only for the moderns, but for the older poets such a system is wholly inadequate. A scheme that accounts for the accentual as well as temporal aspects of a poem is necessary. At the suggestion of Professor Francis Magoun of Harvard, I have adopted the system developed by Thomson in his *Rhythm of Speech* (1924) as a means for a better picture of Middle English Verse on which I have been at work; I have found it equally useful for the modern period. It is flexible. A | before the syllable indicates a strong stress, a broken bar ⋮ a weaker one. A three-eight time signature or multiple thereof fits English poetry very well. I have not attempted the subtleties illustrated by Thomson in his important work. An iamb appears as ♪♩. It has been customary to speak of the basic iambic pattern counterpointed with the rhythms of speech. I have myself made such statements, but I now realize it was double-talk, and I here abjure it.

My thanks are due to many persons. One of the most suffering has been Mr. Martin Scholten, himself an excellent poet and one thoroughly conversant with the period covered in this volume. My thanks are due for different reasons to Miss Marigene Valiquette, a most capable secretary, and to Elizabeth Davies Gould, pianist and composer, who verified my musical notation. I owe a great debt, too, to the staffs of the University of Toledo, Toledo Public, New York Public, Widener Memorial

Libraries, and particularly to Mrs. Ivah R. Sweeney for her kindness relative to the holograph material in the Poetry Collection of the Lockwood Memorial Library (Univ. of Buffalo). Although an examination of this material gave me nothing I did not suspect to exist, it did corroborate many conclusions which I had reached independently.

Introduction

IN the Introduction to *Some Modern American Poets* (1950) I pointed out as one of the reasons for less homogeneity in American poetry than would normally be found in that of England, France, Italy, and other countries, the greater diversities in our culture arising from regional differences. The uniformity of America is a myth. In New England, for example, to cite one minor difference that sometimes leads to charges of snobbery, it is important who your family is; in the West it is important what you are as a person; in the mid-West, one encounters both attitudes with the emphasis, however, on what you are. This different point of view leads to frequent misunderstandings. The poets in the present volume represent all parts of the country, and include one poet with Italian ancestry, one an American by adoption, two whose literary lives have been largely spent abroad. Three of them are from the South but not from the same environments. In fact, the environmental conditions of the present group of poets, both economically as well as geographically, probably differ more widely than did those of the first group.

These differences are reflected in the subject matter of their poetry, just as it is in their diction and prosody. Their attitude toward love, for example, is one instance. Mr. Williams, possessed of an intense sexual vitality and the earthiness of a general practising physician, is frank in his acceptance and treatment; Mr. Ransom is more reticent; Miss Wylie pours out her soul in "heart's-desire" lyrics and sonnets; Mr. Auden takes an attitude in which fidelity to one person is an absent quality. Between these lie the attitudes of the others, and in varying moods, serious, playful, and ironic.

Mr. Aiken and Miss Riding are admittedly philosophical, although I should regard neither as profound thinkers. From one point of view, I think Mr. Pound could also be so considered; although his concern, particularly in *The Cantos*, is more political than philosophical. I have a profound respect for some of Mr. Pound's achievements, but I cannot regard his philosophical, or economic, or political ideas as more than sophomoric. Mr. Allen Tate's best work is political. With him, too, I am often in disagreement. I think I can see the barrenness that he sees and the dehumanizing results of our machine civilization, but I also think I can see more. Mr. Ransom and Mr. Williams are nearer the truth. My work is largely with the children of the persons he looks upon as spiritually barren, and, having a closer contact than he, I can see spiritual stirrings that he cannot. One cannot take a short view and be otherwise than disheartened; a large view reveals germinating qualities that will eventually flower. "Present-day happenings," to quote Mr. Giedion, "are simply the most conspicuous sections of a continuum." Mr. Auden's best work is frankly political. His integrity as an artist in presenting his experiences frequently produces results that are unpleasant. I feel that the experiences from which he must orient his ideas gained from other sources are too narrow to make his generalizations of widespread validity.

Death, as is to be expected, is the subject of many poems. The death-wish and death of children underlie some of Mr. Ransom's best work; it is closely bound up with love and the freeing of the soul in Miss Wylie's; it occurs frequently in the poetry of Mr. Van Doren, but modern poetry offers little that is new, except, of course, as the greater knowledge of our universe makes some of the older ideas untenable. This influence manifests itself with the mid-century poets, however, rather than with most of those who are the subject of this volume.

It seems to me, however, that the modern poet shows a greater eclecticism than does the nineteenth-century one. A wider knowledge of the more experimental work of the painters and musicians, in addition to a deeper appreciation of the masterpieces of the past, is everywhere evident. In the nineteenth century there was a tendency for the different departments of human activity to lose contact with one another. The dangers of this have been realized and our more forward-looking thinkers are struggling to reverse the process. In education, for example, although some of our lesser institutions are still working towards greater specialization, our greater institutions are stressing the harmful effects apparent today in this nineteenth-century tendency. In poetry, too, the reversal among the *avant garde*, particularly, is noticeable. Few poets are more familiar with much of the advanced thinking in science and other seemingly unrelated fields than is Mr. Auden.

Gone, too, is the claim that the professor lives behind cloistered walls. Nothing is more ridiculous and farther from the truth than the usual "movie" concept of the college professor. In the present volume, for example, Mr. Ransom is a poet-professor-critic and Mr. Van Doren a professor-poet, and most of the best critical writing in America is that being done by the members of university faculties. Of the younger poets, many now spend part of their time in the class-room. This is good for poet and student alike.

The greatest difference between the poets of the present volume and those of the earlier, however, is in their craftsmanship. Eight of them are radical in their departure from popular tradition; only four are conservative; Mr. Van Doren is the most traditional of the four conservative, with Mr. Aiken, Mr. Hillyer, and Miss Wylie pushing him closely. Some of their work, particularly a few of Mr. Hillyer's songs, has an ageless quality, but much of it will be soon forgotten. Mr. Frost, Mr. Robinson, and Miss Dickinson have exerted the greatest influence on those four. With those who have experimented, it is only natural to assume that much of their early experimentation will be forgotten. There is much good that will remain.

The eight who have departed most radically from the tradition could rightly be thought of as *coterie* poets, a more accurate term, perhaps, than *avant garde* poets. By this I mean that their initial appeal has been to a particular group of readers, small, at least, in the beginning. So to speak of them, however, is not to disparage them. A poet has the inalienable right to make his communication to a limited as well as to a wide audience.

Many of the poets recognized today as among our great ones —Jonson, Donne, Wordsworth, Shelley, to name only a few— were coterie poets at first, although we no longer think of them as such. The limits of the coterie to which they belonged have greatly expanded. Many of Donne's, Jonson's, and Shelley's best poems are still only appreciated by the coteries. On the other hand, I can see no excuse for coterie criticism, because the critic's function is not only to explain the poet, but to explain him from the point of view of the tradition of poetry and from the point of view of those tenets which remain the measuring-sticks of poetry whether we derive our terms of measurement from Aristotle, Longinus, Wordsworth, Coleridge, I. A. Richards, or the so-called "New Criticism." The poet may remain narrow, the critic not. The great difficulty today is with the person who, lacking the perception and taste that can come only from a long, intimate, and studious association with the poetry of the past as well as with that of the present, thinks that to be adept with the critical jargon is all that is necessary to be a capable critic.

Prophecy as to whether the public or coterie poet of today will longer survive is an academic question of little validity. Chaucer, Shakespeare, Spenser, Milton, Pope, Johnson, Byron, the later Tennyson were public poets; Jonson, Donne, Herbert, the early Wordsworth, Keats, Shelley, the early Tennyson—we might even say the early Frost—were coterie poets.

To Mr. Pound, great praise is due for his insistence that poetry must be as carefully written as prose, and for his attempts to free poetry from the manacles of the "goddam iamb." It was not his purpose to work independently of the tradition, but to find new foreign sources for new rhythms. In his best work he has succeeded admirably.

Of the men, Mr. Williams has probably disregarded the tradition more completely than any other poet. Because of this he has been slower to forge a new instrument that would be worthy to place beside the modified instruments with a strongly traditional base. It is Miss Moore and Miss Riding, however, who have in true womanly fashion ignored tradition. Each has done it in her own way—Miss Moore with her light rhymes, Miss Riding by ignoring rhyme. The stanza forms of each are unique. Mr. Ransom, at home with the traditional rhythms, sought and achieved a remarkable freshness by roughening them. Stylistically, Mr. Tate and Mr. Warren owe a great debt to Mr. Ransom. Mr. Auden, one of the finest technicians of them all, and, like Mr. Ransom, thoroughly acclimatized to traditional rhythms, has altered the tradition by giving a lightness and suppleness to his rhythms that are distinctive. He has been enabled to do so as the result of his enlargement of the vocabulary of poetry. In general, the great contribution of the more experimental poets in the present volume has been their success in lightening the rhythms of poetry and freeing them from the elegiac monotony that dominates too much of the poetry of the nineteenth century.

The charge of obscurity has been levelled against much modern poetry; and too often the charge is justified. The causes vary. Mr. Pound's use of ellipsis accounts for much of his. He takes great leaps which his readers cannot encompass. At least, they seem like great leaps; in reality, of course, he has gone safely across on stepping-stones at low tide. When the reader is ready to follow him the tide is in and he finds himself on banks too broad for leaping. Mr. Pound's reading has been more esoteric than that of the average reader, even more so than that of the specialist. Allusions, therefore, that are clear to him are obscure to another. Miss Riding and Mr. Williams have both used ellipsis, but differently. On the other hand, the obscurity of Mr. Aiken is that arising from diffuseness and a concept of form that is unfamiliar. The symphonic form that may be clear to him is blurred for the reader. The obscurity in Mr. Auden arises from his predilection for the rare and unusual word. It is these words that frequently enable him to lighten his rhythms, but, too often, they are not in the dictionary, or if so, only in an unabridged one. His subject matter is sometimes beyond the range of the normal reader. It is ellipsis of a different order from Mr. Pound's, however, that underlies much of the unnecessary obscurity of modern poetry. Mr. Tate's obscurity stems, I think, from his constant attempts to make his diction do what a passionate feeling about his subject would do, granted, of course, that the poet is also a craftsman. By repeated revisions and condensations he has too often tortured his phrases into a lack of comprehensibility and robbed them of all spontaneity. At times, a poet cannot escape obscurity. Shakespeare, Donne, and Hopkins often have it when they are working at white heat. Careful analysis will reveal, however, what they were striving to say. But too many young poets, with no thoughts profound or complicated enough to be obscure, have sought obscurity for its own sake. Fortunately, however, there is a movement away from this deplorable tendency.

On the other hand, Miss Riding is frequently obscure because she does not think a poem needs to be understandable. "A woman's method with a material," she says, "is to state only as much of it as may be stated conclusively, a man's to state as much as possible without regard to conclusiveness." I am not sure just what she means, but I think that what is conclusive for her is not enough for a man. In *Americans*, however, where her style is informal and her meaning clear, her observations are superficial and her humour heavy. In her other poetry, however, the unstated part permits the reader to sense depth where, perhaps, there is none. Many of her poems, however, remain complete enigmas to me. Others are profoundly moving.

In their imagery the poets in the present volume are generally fresh. At his best, Mr. Aiken has a keenly perceptive mind; at his dead-level of monotonously musical verse his images are trite and general. Miss Wylie and Mr. Van Doren would have been the poorer without Aldeberan, a geographical entity that serves them both with inexactness. The images of Mr. Williams, Mr. Ransom, and Mr. Warren are in many ways the most rewarding.

xviii

Miss Moore is the most refreshing in the way she has sought and found the precise image suitable for her purpose.

Many of the poets have striven for new forms. Miss Wylie, and Messrs. Van Doren, Tate, and Hillyer have made extensive use of the sonnet form. They prove conclusively how difficult a medium the sonnet is, and younger poets should heed the warning their failures give. They are workmanlike. Not much more can be said for them.

Although the present age has frequently been called that of the short rather than of the long poem, many of the poets in the present volume have attempted long poems. A long poem is clearly beyond the scope of Mr. Hillyer. The most successful ones in my opinion are Mr. Williams' "Paterson" and Mr. Warren's "The Ballad of Billie Potts." Good as are many parts of *The Cantos* I can only view them as a colossal failure. Mr. Van Doren's efforts are failures on a lesser scale and of a different kind, and Mr. Auden is only partially successful.

Self-criticism has been strangely absent from much modern poetry. This may partially be due to the fact that so many of the poets who may be said to be coterie poets have been influenced by *coterie* criticism. Mr. Ransom and Miss Moore, being strongly self-critical, have saved the reader much pain and anguish. I wish that Mr. Williams, Miss Riding, or Mr. Aiken had had a portion of this same self-critical faculty, although the reader should not minimize this quality in Mr. Williams.

The foregoing statements comprise, of course, only part of the truth. The individual essays themselves will correct and modify their boldness or presumptive dogmatism. A word should be said, however, about the extant criticism of the poets under consideration. Much of the criticism in our organs of fairly extensive distribution is incompetent and perfunctory. We have no publication comparable to the London *Times Literary Supplement*. Our best criticism appears in the smaller or so-called "little" magazines which are dedicated to a definite point of view. This is, of course, understandable since it is those with a definite point of view who are willing to provide the money for one or two years' publication. I have already spoken of the dangers of this restricted perspective. Even when the small magazine opens its pages to all points of view, however, the appeal is to the specialist rather than to the common reader. In such criticism, the writer often mistakes crabbedness and obscurity for profundity. It is unfortunate that so many persons have been deluded into mistaking one for the other. Obscurity in criticism arises only from imperfectly crystallized ideas. Clarity does not imply the lack of perceptiveness. I feel strongly about this matter because I feel it is dangerous to the cause of poetry. One critic, for example, has gained a high reputation, and yet no one to whom I have talked about him can tell me what he is trying to say. If readers demand clarity they will get it. On the other hand, some of the critics are beginning to realize the dangers. Mr. Jarrell, for example, seems to be facing and conquering the dangers.

For some account of the younger poets not included in this volume I should like to refer the reader to *Mid-Century American Poets*, edited by John Ciardi, which gives a comprehensive glance at what is going on. Unfortunately, the volume, in its prose statements, also contains much critical nonsense; and it is apparent from some of the comments of the contributors that they were aware that it would. It is obvious that the same tendencies are apparent in those who have not yet arrived as in those who have reached or passed their peak. We have the traditionalist, the moderate, and the radical innovator. One thing, however, is all too clear in this volume—the unevenness of the selection of almost every one of the contributors. Yet there is much good in the volume, in spite of the lack of self-criticism evident throughout. Mr. Peter Viereck, Mr. Theodore Roethke, and Miss Muriel Rukeyser give promise of better things to come. Mr. Jarrell and Mr. Shapiro, whom I mentioned with Mr. Lowell and Mr. Horan, in *Some Modern American Poets*, seem to be devoting more of their time to criticism. Or if not, they are giving their poetry a chance to mature. It is only as these younger poets subject themselves to unpitying criticism that they will grow in stature. I should like also to call the reader's attention to the work of a younger colleague of mine, Mr. Martin Scholten, whose first volume, *A Later Shore*, has received favourable critical acclaim. His work, too, is passing from the period of promise to that of accomplishment, and bears watching. His four years in India have profoundly altered his thinking, first generated against an Iowan background.

Deplore as people will the decline of poetry, I think they are wrong in their facts. Never before has poetry been read as poetry so much as it is being read at the present time. In increasing numbers readers are turning to poetry as an art in which all the ingredients are fused into a carefully integrated whole in order to achieve significant form, rather than for the purpose of finding their own ideas sweetly and rhythmically expressed. Approaching poetry in this way will be bound to have healthful results.

In my previous volume I said that Mr. Frost, Hart Crane, and Mr. Wallace Stevens would determine the present poetic heights in America. I should like to extend the list to include Mr. Ransom. Now that he has become an American citizen, Mr. Auden certainly belongs there, if for no other reason than his sheer metrical virtuosity. The late work of Mr. Williams, particularly *Paterson*, and the deeper quality of that of Miss Moore make them serious contenders for a more prominent position among our leading poets.

A careful reading of our modern poets will do much to help us to a clearer and finer appreciation of our older poets. I am speaking not of what our older poets tell us but of how they tell us what they do. Their rhythms more nearly approach the flexibility of modern rhythms than those of the poetry of any other period. To appreciate their great flexibility, however, we must first adjust our ears to nuance denied the person nurtured on nineteenth-century rhythms. The professor-critic is apt to be most at fault here, although I know one prominent English anthologist who boasted he knew nothing of modern poetry. What he did not realize was that æsthetically speaking he was making an anthology for the mid-century that did not fit the facts of the period. With the knowledge of our present we shall possibly see that, prosodically speaking, the fourteenth, fifteenth, and sixteenth centuries were not so dark as the literary historian would sometimes have us believe, and that the seventeenth is unbelievably rich. To be able to do even this much, modern poetry will have more than justified itself.

Dr. William Carlos Williams
1883—

D<small>R. WILLIAM CARLOS WILLIAMS</small> has never
been a popular poet, nor is he likely to become one. The reason
is obvious. He taxes the reader more than the general reader
wishes to be taxed. Except in his first immature volume—*The
Tempers* (1913)—he has eschewed the traditional aids of rhyme,
regularly recurring rhythms, traditional stanza forms, and a
music arising from the felicitous juxtaposition of words. Instead,
he has struggled toward and has finally achieved in *Paterson* a
line that springs from the rhythms of American speech. Other
poets have achieved such a line while still employing these traditional aids; he, after much struggle, has finally wrought a line
with the desired inner tension without them. Read chronologically
his poetry mirrors the obvious as well as subtle changes that take
place as a person progresses from youth to age, especially when
that person is a physician whose practice keeps him constantly
in touch with the world of people. Useful as the psychological
approach may be, however, it has little to do with a correct
evaluation of his work from the æsthetic point of view, our
present problem.

The change from the traditional to more unique forms begins
in his second volume, *Transitional* (1915), and is a desirable
change, because the poems in *The Tempers* (1913) are of a poor,
unpromising quality. We find bad Browning, little sense of the
musical potential of words in juxtaposition, little felicitous
handling of stanza forms, no actual touch with life. As absolute
poetry, except for an occasional lovely line, they are worthless.

From his second volume, "Le Médecin Malgré Lui" points

the way his better work is to take. He knows what he is writing about and he communicates to the reader through the sheer honesty of accurate detail a vivid picture of a laboratory in disarray. A scientist would be deeply impressed by the accuracy of each detail of the description regardless of its poetic worth. Personally, I feel no tension in the lines, and see no advantage in setting it up as poetry rather than as prose, say, as one of his Improvisations. This inner tension first appears in *Al Que Quiere* (1917) where the poet's deeply sensuous nature is readily apparent in such poems as "Sub Terra," "Pastoral," "Love Song," "Winter Sunset," "Winter Quiet," "Good Night," "Smells," "To a Solitary Disciple," and "Dedication for a Plot of Ground." These are not Dr. Williams' best poems. They lack the quiet force and greater concentration of many of his later ones, but they are, I think, a good starting-point for the person unfamiliar with his work. They are still strongly subjective in the manner of a good lyric and do not tax the powers of the reader as does much of his later work. They have youthful ardour, warmth, and a surging vitality. The poet has not yet begun to make extensive use of ellipsis nor to write the type of poem to which the term "objectivist" has been applied.

Nothing so clearly indicates Dr. Williams' creative powers as the fact that he is not content to repeat himself. His work changes because of inner necessity, because he is constantly striving to perfect the instrument by means of which he can relieve himself of the strain under which he has always lived. I think he might call it his search for "local assertion." *Sour Grapes* (1921) mirrors the change. There are the subjective "April," "Blueflags," "Complaint," and "To a Friend Concerning Several Ladies," and the objective "Blizzard," "The Poor" and others.

It is poems of this latter type of which the *Collected Poems: 1921-1931* largely consists. Time has, I think, supported Mr. Ezra Pound's early appraisal of this volume: "Bill's worst work. . . . But there is some damn good stuff there." It is this volume that has tended to restrict his appeal to those who admire him as the founder of the "objectivist" school, the basic tenets of which appear to be that a poem has little to do with the sound of the language, that it is not concerned with the explicit communication by traditional poetic aids of the feeling of the poet toward an object, but that the poetry is in the object itself, and the poet's function is, by means of essentially anti-poetic language ("scientific" might be a better term), so to describe the object that the reader will, by an imaginative act, create from the dispassionate description the same emotional reaction to the object as that experienced by the poet. Naturally, this demands a more definite creative act on the part of the reader than most readers can or are willing to give. In his recent *Autobiography*, his definition of "objectivist" differs somewhat from the foregoing. The poem is an object "that in itself formally presents its case and its meaning by the very form it assumes," and as such "should be so treated and controlled," but in a contemporary manner. Out of his words the poet was to create a new form, the purpose of which was to serve as an antidote "to the bare image haphazardly presented in loose verse." If this is what the group really meant, there was nothing basically new in the idea.

Or, it may be explained in another way. Dr. Williams' purpose in writing "objectivist" verse is essentially one of values. "The true value," he has said in *Improvisations,* "is that peculiarity which gives an object a character by itself. The association or sentimental value is the false. Its imposition is due to lack of imagination, to an easy lateral sliding. The attention has been held too rigid on the one plane instead of following a more flexible, jagged resort." The difficulty with his earlier experiments in "objectivist" poetry is that too often the "object" being described is characterless or trivial. Naturally, the associational value is often implied. "The Red Wheelbarrow," for example, so frequently cited, is a case in point. For Dr. Williams it has a definite character and significance. For the average reader it has neither. Had there been more poems like "The Source," "The Red Lily," "The Bull," "The Sun Bathers," and "The Winds," and fewer like "This is Just to Say" and most of the others, *Collected Poems: 1921-1931* might have had a wider appeal.

Hardy sought to see the beauty in the ugliness of life. Dr. Williams has sought it where Hardy did, but he has also sought it in nature in its most sensuous and undramatic moods, in the country as well as down deserted streets and in back alleys, in the common-placeness and vulgarity of the American scene, particularly that of the lower middle and lower classes. He has also sought it in the little unremembered acts of kindness and of love. He has sought it within himself and his intimate contacts both as lusty male and as physician capable of compassion; he has sought it in the solution of an æsthetic problem from which will emerge spiritual satisfaction; and he has sought it—particularly of late—in the political scene. More specifically, he has sought it in a young sycamore, a red wheelbarrow, a severed cod head lifting and falling between the green stones, a bull, a waitress, a crowd at the ball game, a woman in front of a bank, or in a host of other places. The tangible, everyday world and the workaday people are the stuff of his poetry. At no time does he stray from reality, although his deeply emotional attitude towards this reality would place him in the category of the romantics, specifically among the men of feeling. By no means, however, should he be confused with the sentimentalist. "The Storm," "Against the Sky," and "The Yellow Chimney," although different in mood, would help define the nature of his romanticism. In all three he selects only the most relevant details and carefully excludes any tendency to moralize.

Dr. Williams' attitude toward poetry is similar to his attitude toward love. He confessed to his wife his erotics with other women, believing that from them finer relations with her developed. "It is in the continued and violent refreshing of the idea," he said, "that love and good writing have their security." No reader could ever doubt the fierceness of his integrity. Or, as he has said in his *Autobiography*: "Men have given the direction to my life and women have always supplied the energy." He has Wordsworth's eye for significant detail without his tendency to deduce some universal truth from the object. This is not to say that there is no universal truth, but that the reader must find that truth for himself from the outline provided by the poet. Here is "The Yellow Chimney":

> *There is a plume*
> *of fleshpale*
> *smoke upon the blue*
>
> *sky. The silver*
> *rings that*
> *strap the yellow*
>
> *brick stack at*
> *wide intervals shine*
> *in this amber*
>
> *light—not*
> *of the sun not of*
> *the pale sun but*
>
> *his born brother*
> *the*
> *declining season.*

It is obvious, of course, that when as much responsibility rests on the reader as Dr. Williams places there, the chances of failure of response on the part of the reader are greater than if the poet had made use of the traditional tools for controlling that response. The young reader will overstress the importance of poems which lie within his range of experience; the older reader, those which lie within his. But when has that ever been any different? In my own case it is such poems as "The Forgotten City," "Chanson," "The Well Disciplined Bargeman," "The Mind's Games," "A Place (Any Place) to Transcend All Places," "Approach to a City," "The Old House," "The Clouds," and "The Seafarer" that afford me the greatest pleasure. Not only

5

do most of the earlier poems lack significance, but even in *The Collected Later Poems* I find unsatisfactory such poems as "For a Low Voice," "Lustspiel," "To Be Hungry Is to Be Great," "Navajo," and "Raindrops on a Briar." Many others have interest.

His method of introducing the details that he thinks necessary for creating a mood of correspondence in his reader is often subtle, making use of definition by negation. The tree of "A Place (Any Place) to Transcend All Places" affords an interesting example:

> *leaves filling,*
> *making, a tree (but*
> *wait) not just leaves,*
> *leaves of one design that*
> *make a certain design,*
> *no two alike, not like*
> *the locust either, next in line,*
> *nor the Rose of Sharon, in*
> *the pod-stage, near it—a*
> *tree! Imagine it! Pears*
> *philosophically hard. Nor*
> *thought that is from*
> *branches on a root, from*
> *an acid soil, with scant*
> *grass about the bole*
> *where it breaks through.*

Certainly he is Wordsworth's man speaking to men, and he is more alive to the sensuous world about him than are most. The reader who will not let himself be deterred by an unfamiliar technique cannot escape having his eyes opened to new beauties about him; and to new ugliness. But those beauties come not with the first, but with repeated readings; often with the second, but more often with the third. A younger generation trained to accept without misgiving Bartok, as well as Bach, Beethoven, and Brahms, will be less disconcerted by his anti-

6

poetic rhythms than the older whose training lacked Bartok. Or a reader who is content to submerge himself in Dr. Williams' poetry for a concentrated period will soon train his ear to hear his music. In *Paterson*, in particular, the music is often of a haunting beauty. It is here that he achieves his greatest success. I shall reserve *Paterson*, however, for later discussion.

The question that has constantly confronted me while steeping myself in Dr. Williams' poetry is whether a more traditional form, employing the usual devices of rhyme and a more regular rhythm in various stanzas of regular or irregular design, would enhance his communication. Because it is the obvious lack of these aids to communicating emotion that keeps many readers from his work. I have tried to envisage some of his shorter poems. I think Dr. Williams knew what he was about. The trivial poems might have gained a measure of popularity, but they would remain trivial. And no one knows better than the poet the little satisfaction to be derived from the praise of the uncritical. The good poems would lose some of their basic integrity if cast in any other mould, and it is their uncompromising integrity that makes the reader return to them until he finds other qualities.

Since the lyrical strain is carefully excluded, for reasons of temperament no doubt, but since most of the poems are divided into stanzaic patterns, the question arises as to the poet's types of metrical lines. In instance after instance, I have experimented with a poem by writing it out as prose and then so reading it. The poetry remained. Why then, were they written as prose poems? As if the poet were himself aware of the problem he has given us "A Crystal Maze" in which the 35 lines of Part I are condensed to 26 lines of Part II. Lines set up in one way in Part I are set up differently in Part II. For example:

> *Hard, hard to learn—*
> *that love, through bars and against*
> *back strokes, is to make mine*
> *each by his own gesture—the toss*
> *of a cigarette—*

giving, laying himself bare,
offering, watching
for its flash of certainty in
the confused onslaught

becomes with some interesting substitutions and omissions:

Hard, hard to learn—
that love, against bars and
counter strokes is mine
each by his own gesture—
the toss of a cigarette—
laying himself bare
offering, watching
for a flash of certainty
in the confused onslaught—

An interesting instance of the care given to an apparently effortless poem is his treatment of "The Sleeping Brute." There are fourteen versions of this poem in the Poetry Collection of the Lockwood Memorial Library in Buffalo. Here is the poem:

For three years at evening
the sparrow has come
under the roof to sleep.

What has this to do
with the war in Europe? For
three years winter

and summer the same sparrow
with covered head
darkly among the grey shadows.

The first version was not divided into stanzas and was less spare than the final. In the second version we can see the poet experimenting with the proper division of lines describing the bird, lines which were later deleted entirely. Versions three and four still concern themselves with accuracy of diction, rearrangement

8

of phrases, details which in the final version disappear. The three-line stanza first appears in the fifth version which contains six stanzas. In the sixth version, the poet returns to a three-section division, and in the middle section he is undecided whether or not the line "What has this to do with the war in Europe?" should be broken after "with." In the seventh version he suggests breaking the line after "do." In the eighth he returns to the three-line stanza; the ninth restores the poem to the three sections of the sixth version; the tenth divides it into four-line stanzas; the eleventh deletes many details and reduces the poem to three four-line stanzas; the twelfth is a fair copy of the eleventh; the thirteenth is a reduction of the poem to three three-line stanzas, again with four instances of experimentation with the line divisions; the fourteenth introduces many changes. The following is the typescript:

For three years the sparrow
has come winter and summer
under the porch roof to sleep.

What has this to do with
the war in Europe? For three
years winter and summer

the same sparrow under
the porch roof upon a jutting
edge among the grey shadows.

The poet has made the pencil jottings which heeded lead to the final draft bearing his signature.

What Dr. Williams has done so extensively with this one poem, he has done to a lesser degree with almost every poem. The differences are subtle but sure. A lesser craftsman would have been satisfied with rhythms less delicately modulated.

Quite obviously the basic idea of his music cannot be indicated by the usual marks of stress and unstress. A musical notation affords a more accurate picture. Let us examine a passage from

"The Clouds," and it is apparent that his stresses are lighter than customary:

Tragic outlines

and the bodies of horses, mindfilling — but

visible! against the invisible; actual against

the imagined and the concocted; unspoiled by hands

and unshaped also by them but caressed by sight only,

moving among them, not that that propels

the eyes from under, while it blinds

What Dr. Williams has here achieved is a passage of subtle music with a fundamental prose rhythm. Too often, however, the subtle music is missing. He best succeeds in *Paterson*. Such passages, for example, as that beginning "We sit and talk" (I, ii, p. 35), "Without invention nothing is well spaced" (II, i, p. 65), and, particularly, "The descent beckons" (II, iii, p. 96), grow in beauty with each reading. The poet's best work requires, as I have suggested, at least three readings before the subtlety of the form begins clearly to reveal itself.

It is only in the later work that I feel the poet has succeeded in forging a musical instrument from the speech rhythms which were his models. It is only here that one experiences any sense of the inevitableness of his diction, or that the line divisions are themselves inevitable.

Although the poet forgoes rhyme except on a few occasions —and those occasions indicate that he was wise to forgo it—he does make use of other devices, ellipsis, as I have said, being one of the most obvious, as it is in the poetry of Mr. Pound. When properly used it is effective. Too often, however, it is employed to cover the poet's inability to meet an imaginative challenge. This is true of the earlier rather than the later work. Dr. Williams has made a proper as well as improper use of it, the latter chiefly in his early poems. "At the Ball Game," and "Stop: Go" illustrate the device. Whether it is successful or not in the following passage, the reader must judge for himself:

> *a green truck*
> *dragging a concrete mixer*
> *passes*
> *in the street—*
> *the clatter and true sound*
> *of verse—*

The poet is immensely successful, however, in his use of similes where he is accurate and contemporary. The horse, for example, blows "fog from his nostrils like fumes from the twin exhausts of a car." (Why does the poet make five lines out of the quotation?) Or the extended one about infra-red rays from "The Mirrors." Or the statement on deftness from "Aigeltenger":

> *Deftness stirs in the cells*
> *of Aigeltenger's brain which flares*
> *like ribbons round an electric fan.*

The early poems are rich in simile and metaphor, and often where one would least expect it, in alliteration. His predominant figure, however, is metaphor, and it is everywhere apparent.

Dr. Williams' major claim to poetic laurels will finally depend, however, on the success or failure of his long poem *Paterson*. In "Paterson: the Falls" and in the "Author's Note," prefixed to the volume containing the first three books, the poet provides a clue to the poem.

"*Paterson* [writes Dr. Williams] is a long poem in four parts —that a man in himself is a city, beginning, seeking, achieving, and concluding his life in ways which the various aspects of a city may embody—if imaginatively conceived—any city, all the details of which may be made to voice his most intimate convictions. Part One introduces the elemental character of the place. The Second Part comprises the modern replicas. Three will seek a language to make them vocal, and Four, the river below the falls, will be reminiscent of episodes—all that any one man may achieve in a lifetime."

The problem of form of this essentially autobiographical poem was one that the poet had pondered long, and for excellent reasons. He wanted an "image large enough to embody the whole knowable world" about him, and he realized that the "isolated observations and experiences needed pulling together to gain 'profundity.' " New York City was out of his perspective and he wanted a city on a river. Paterson with its falls gave him what he needed—the symbol that would embrace the diverse aspects he thought necessary if the poem were to have the integrity of the subject. He believed with good authority that the poet's business was to deal with particulars, not vague categories, and to discover the universal in these particulars. He realized that thinking man is a complex organism moulded and influenced by many forces, and in turn moulding and influencing others. Since his subject was a unique man, rather than man in general, the form itself must be unique. It called for a new poetry. He must be a "maker" in the strict sense of the word. He not only had to fulfil all "the requirements of art, and yet [make it] new, in the sense that in the very lay of the syllables Paterson as Paterson would be discovered." The very sound must bolster the uncompromising integrity of the poet. This is not the integrity of a person who has lived away from the masses, but the more solid one of a person who has moved among the publicans and sinners and has not been swerved from his purpose by them, although they are part and parcel of his thinking.

The Preface to Book I reveals a mastery of his idiom that is

12

not often apparent in the shorter poems; and by this perfected idiom, the communication of a passion and emotion that is absent from the earlier work. Recognizing that our knowledge is limited to our own complexities, he presents a picture of man, largely as a product of environment.

> *Yet there is*
> *no return: rolling up out of chaos,*
> *a nine months' wonder, the city*
> *the man, an identity—it can't be*
> *otherwise—an*
> *interpenetration, both ways. Rolling*
> *up! obverse, reverse;*
> *the drunk the sober; the illustrious*
> *the gross; one. In ignorance*
> *a certain knowledge and knowledge*
> *undispersed, its own undoing.*

He does not exalt the literary man above others, especially the literary man who is a writer of stale poems.

It is in Book I, "The Delineaments of the Giants," that the reader will encounter his first major difficulty. Interspersed among the passages of poetry are prose passages that at first glance seem irrelevant. Careful reading, however, reveals that they are integrated with the preceding verses, but provide details that would be inappropriate as verse, usually because of their undue length. The first prose passage, for example, is directly related to one of the women of

> *A man like a city and a woman like a flower*
> *—who are in love. Two women. Three women.*
> *Innumerable women, each like a flower.*
> > *But*
> *only one man—like a city.*

The second prose passage describing the finding of pearls in mussels at Notch Brook near Paterson, is an elaboration of

"Pearls at her ankles"; the third one, of the wonders that satisfied those that "craved the miraculous"; and so on throughout the poem. Often they are elusive and require the closest attention to the text which has a density much greater than is found in any of the earlier work.

By the device of thinking of Paterson the city as a man lying dreaming and by closely merging himself with Paterson the man, the poet has solved the technical problem of giving form to a mass of material difficult to synthesize. Dr. Williams is fully aware that the poet is a product of his environment as well as an influence on that environment. The waters approaching the brink of the falls are likened to the way thoughts jostle one another in a man's mind. The thoughts arise from the populace, and the poet's philosophy was formed from experience rather than abstract speculation. Or, to quote,

> *Inside the bus one sees*
> *his thoughts sitting and standing. His*
> *thoughts alight and scatter—*

He realizes that he can never understand these people—"the equation is beyond solution"—but is fully aware that few of them attain a full life. Just as on all abstract matters, he communicates his thoughts on youth and age by specific illustrations. As he repeats, there are "no ideas but in things." Section II of Part I further breaks down the subject and the reader begins to sense the autobiographic nature of many of the episodes. Many sections are difficult because of the inability to grasp the stark honesty of the poet. Realizing that knowledge comes late, he has only begun to grasp the "know clearly . . . whence [he draws his breath] or how to employ it clearly—if not well."

Section III of Part I is the defiant attitude of a man who is alive, continually growing, vibrant with the knowledge he has gleaned from his contacts with humanity toward the myth of youth as a golden age. It is only natural that such a person would be antagonistic toward the sterile professors who in their teaching fail to give their students the tools by which to live. It is these that

> *block the release*
> *that should cleanse and assume*
> *prerogatives as a private recompense.*
> *Others are also at fault because*
> *they do nothing.*

The poet feels himself alone. He cannot run toward the peripheries, but life's mystery for him resides in the surrounding reality of

> *Tenement windows, sharp edged, in which*
> *no face is seen—though curtainless, into*
> *which no more than birds and insects look or*
> *the moon stares, concerning which they dare*
> *look back, by times.*

Part II, called "Sunday in the Park," employs a device that gives unity to a series of free associations. The time is late spring, a Sunday afternoon. The poet joins the crowd, is aware of them as individuals as well as members of a class, thinking specifically of the awkwardness of young girls,

> *. . . the ugly legs of the young girls*
> *pistons too powerful for delicacy*

After looking back over the city, he resumes his walking. At first aware of the nature of the terrain and of the vegetation, his mind drifts to the activity of walking itself, then to one of the erotic episodes in his life. He recalls specifically parts of a letter he had received from a woman who was anxious to write poetry but wanted a greater experience of life. This musing is interrupted by the welling from the sub-conscious to the conscious of the opening of Elizabeth Barrett Browning's sonnet, "How do I Love Thee?" Without transition he is then recalled to

15

the crowds about him and reports some of their vapid conversation. From this he drifts back into the past of Paterson and thinks of the tragic circumstances from a time when there was no park. He shifts back to the present, aware that this is the season of bird-mating, watches the birds, thinks again of love, and recalls further passages from the letter of the woman. Each of these transitions is indicated by the one word "Walking—." As Part II progresses, the texture of the poem becomes richer, his observations keener. There is a steady movement from the concrete to the abstract, from the particular to the general, from the personal to the political.

Since it is not my purpose to give an exegesis of the poem, but only to point out the method of approach to the poem, I shall refrain from further analysis. Parts III and IV have abundant riches of their own, although, from my point of view, III is richer than IV, and the technique is the same. The important fact is that the poem has a richness that completely eludes the easy reader. It contains passages of as fine poetry as we have so far had in America. But it is difficult, and even with careful re-reading not at all times clear. Some knowledge of the biographical facts underlying the poem will throw much light on it. We need both notes and a commentary. But above all we need patience to learn to hear the music—often impassioned music—that is in every section of the poem. After a long struggle to forge a new instrument that would give forth music close to man's everyday world, Dr. Williams has finally succeeded. Just how difficult that music is can be easily determined by steeping oneself in that of Dr. Williams and then that of another poet working in the great tradition—Auden, for example. Dr. Williams' best work does not suffer in the comparison.

Many times during the present study of Dr. Williams' poetry I have been reminded of the old truism that a person does not know what he likes, he likes what he knows. *Paterson* has been the most recalcitrant of the poems in revealing itself, but in the end it is the richest. Dr. Williams' work can best be read in selection, because he has not always been as self-critical of his work before publication as he should have been. Much that he has published has little value. On the other hand, a careful reader of *The Later Collected Poems* and *Paterson* will find abundant recompense for the effort he must expend to recognize their worth. And when the recompense is adequate when is the effort better spent?

Ezra Pound
1885—

MR. EZRA POUND is essentially a poet for poets. Not only has he given generously of himself over the years to any young poet of talent who sought his aid, but he has given them poems from which, without acknowledgement, they can and have purloined subtleties of which they were themselves incapable. He has taught them, as well as the serious general reader, to have an increased appreciation of the musical sentence. His critical faculty, keenly perceptive of the larger conception as well as of the minutiæ, enabled him to help men like T. S. Eliot, James Joyce, Lawrence Binyon, and numerous others. It matters little whether the reader agrees or disagrees with some of his experiments, but he must admit that his influence has been a healthy one for American poetry. The intelligent general reader, however, who is not interested in metrical experiment *qua* experiment, or in work that is a storehouse from which to borrow, will be attracted to some poems, repelled by others, and indifferent to many.

He owes, however, a great debt to Mr. Pound in that at a time when poetry was at a low ebb in America, he looked upon it as an art with a technique and media, and recognized that it must be in a constant flux if it were to live. He realized that the iambic pentameter had been overworked and sought to break its dominance by a return to an analysis of more primitive systems. Years later he felt that "the best *mechanism* for breaking up the stiffness and literary idiom *is* a different metre; the goddam iambic magnetizes certain verbal sequences." It is unfortunate that his attack was delayed until the present century. Had it occurred earlier it might have prevented some of the

18

elaborate baseless theories about Chaucer's versification by Child, Ten Brink, and others, who were under the spell of the iambic pentameter line, a line unknown in Chaucer's day. Mr. Pound sought the new rhythms, as Chaucer had done, by a careful study of continental writers. He also sought to write natural speech and to avoid the archaisms in which he had "wallowed in [his] vealish years."

It is difficult for the reader of modern poetry to realize that in 1915 "talking seriously and without parade" as a dictum of poetry was not a generally accepted one. In a letter to Harriet Monroe (*Letters*, 48, 49) on the requirements of poetry, Mr. Pound expressed ideas which are now accepted as axiomatic—it should be well written, simple, and hard; its rhythms should be tight, meaningful, and those of speech; it should avoid bookish words, periphrases, inversions, clichés, and set phrases; it should be objective and straightforward.

He summarized these briefly in a letter to Iris Barry:

"The whole art is divided into:

(*a*) concision, or style, or saying what you mean in the fewest and clearest words.

(*b*) the actual necessity for creating or constructing something; or presenting an image, or enough images of concrete things arranged to stir the reader."—(*Letters*, p. 90).

It is obvious that poetry was not an easy art, but one that required adequate preparation. The poet need not only study the classics but needed to develop his own idiom. By knowing the classics, he was in no danger of imitating the false ones. They were "acids to gnaw through the thongs and bull-hides with which we are tied by our schoolmasters. They are the antiseptics. They are almost the only antiseptics against the contagious imbecility of mankind." It is of little importance at the moment whether or not we agree with him specifically in what he terms some of the classics; theoretically he was right, just as he was right in thinking that there "is no democracy in the arts."

Mr. Pound was correct, too, in many of his castigations of professors. It is still true that too many follow the "safe" way of giving the student the facts *about* literature rather than the facts *of* literature. They suffer from what he called "anemia of guts," whereas some of his contemporaries writing poetry suffered from "anemia of education." Believing that "the definite vacancy is in melodic validity" he attempted to fill that vacancy.

Before examining Mr. Pound's positive contributions to "melodic validity," let us briefly consider his subject matter, because it is the uncongeniality of much of the subject matter that is a real stumbling block for the general reader. Foreign literatures have appealed to Mr. Pound, and he has borrowed from them extensively. His borrowings are often little more than free translations. His chief interest in the Provençal, Chinese, and Latin literatures was the possibilities they offered the poet seeking new rhythms. Scholars have criticized Mr. Pound for the inaccuracy of his translations. I think he worked in the tradition of the Elizabethan translators rather than that of the present day where a rigid adherence to the text is accepted as axiomatic. He sought to capture the spirit of his original. Occasionally, as in Propertius, the reader senses a strong affinity between the translator and the translated, but there is rarely a transmutation of the material into something contemporary and significant such as we find in Shakespeare's "translation" of his sources.

The reader feels, therefore, that much of his poetry, in spite of the occasional brilliance of his technical achievement, is anachronistic, even sterile. None of the poems in the early *Personæ* has a modern subject, although the versification is often decidedly so. Since the poet does not reinterpret these old subjects, what is the purpose of reviving them in modern verse? Does this not perhaps suggest that Mr. Pound's egoism gets the better of the artist in him? What interests him should, he thinks, interest the general reader. But it fails to. It is significant that his most widely known poem is the early "The Ballad of the Goodly Fere," although no critic would rank it as his best. It is one of the few, however, with a subject of wide general appeal.

When Mr. Pound does consider a contemporary subject and sets aside some of his objectivity, his spleen gets the better of his artistic sense and he arouses little sympathy in his readers. This is not as true of the poems in *Ripostes* as of those in *Lustra*. In the latter, he rages against those who are better off than he. His is the unhealthy immature attitude of a person who rails against society in which he cannot find acceptance, and in which, if he could, he would not be at ease. "The Rest," "Les Millwin," "Salutation," "Meditatio," "To Dives" forecast themes that will receive more elaborate treatment in *The Cantos*, in conjunction with the themes treated in all his translations. In the *Ripostes*, "Silet," "Portrait d'une Femme," "N.Y.," "Quies," "The Needle," and "The Plunge," he neither rails nor is he as objective as he is to become. Metrically, these poems have a more traditional music than many in *Personæ* or *Lustra*.

Although many of the poems comprising *Cathay* are of little general interest from the point of view of subject matter, certain ones have a timelessness and a universality. Such are "The Beautiful Toilet," "The River-Merchant's Wife: a Letter," "Exile's Letter," and "A Ballad of the Mulberry Road." To appreciate these poems, the reader should read them as original poems. Mr. Pound frankly admitted that he did not really know enough to read Japanese or that he could do "more than spell out ideograms *very* slowly with a dictionary." Nor when he did *Cathay* did he have any "inkling of the technique of sound" which he was later convinced "*must* exist or have existed in Chinese poetry."

He realized the failure of his attempt to interest readers in troubadour work of twelfth-century Provence. Although he had hoped to use its subject matter as Browning had used the matter of Renaissance Italy, his imagination was not sufficiently powerful to use it with his own personality, thereby giving it a modern significance. He was interested in Arnaut and Guido as "psychological, almost physiological diagnosticians." The emotions

21

on which they exercised their diagnostic powers have little contemporary interest.

The two poems of Mr. Pound most admired by his readers are "Homage to Sextus Propertius," and "Hugh Selwyn Mauberley." Both are more successful than his others in breaking through, partially at least, the objectivity he thought so important. The common theme is the situation of the artist out of sympathy with his time. The underlying purpose of "Homage to Sextus Propertius" was to present certain emotions vital to Mr. Pound in 1917, faced, as he said, "with the infinite and ineffable imbecility of the British Empire, as they were to Propertius some centuries earlier, when faced with the infinite and ineffable imbecility of the Roman Empire. These emotions are defined largely, but not entirely, in Propertius' own terms. If the reader does not find relation to life defined in the poem, he may conclude," he continues, "that I have been unsuccessful in my endeavour. I certainly omitted no means of definition that I saw open to me, including shortenings, cross cuts, implications derivable from other writings of Propertius, as for example the 'Ride to Lanuvium,' from which I have taken a colour or tone but no direct or entire expression." "Homage," however, is less successful than "Mauberley," in spite of the brilliance of its prosody. One of the reasons for this is that it states the theme less directly. It would be wrong, however, to confuse the poet with Mauberley just as it would be to confuse Eliot with Prufrock. Mr. Pound realized that "Mauberley" would be "merely a translation of the 'Homage to Sextus Propertius,'" for such as couldn't understand the latter. Some of Mr. Pound's finest writing occurs in "Mauberley," and already many younger poets have been influenced by his rhythms. I even sense his influence on Mr. Ransom.

A discussion of the subject matter of *The Cantos*, Mr. Pound's most ambitious venture, of which eighty-four have so far been published, is appropriate at this point. To do so, however, would necessitate a retracing of our steps when we consider his technical achievement in this work, which he described in January, 1927, as "really LONG, endless, leviathanic." It is not Mr. Pound's subject matter that has intrinsic value. Let us, therefore, subordinate its discussion to that dealing with its technical aspects.

From the point of view of Mr. Pound's technical virtuosity I can admire much that he has accomplished. In a period of shoddy, loose, sentimental over-writing, he not only realized the danger of such writing but he sought to influence others to give "hard light" and "clear edges" to their work. He likewise sought and succeeded in giving it to his own.

His early experiments with rhythms were not revolutionary, but they were a definite break from the too strongly iambic beat. The opening of "Na Audiart" illustrates the nature of his experiments. Although I have generally restricted my scansion to 3/8 measure, the usual measure in most poetry since the fourteenth century, I have at times been forced to a combination of 3/8 and 2/4. Certainly, however, the 3/8 dominates:

Though thou well dost wish me ill

Audiart, Audiart

Where thy bodice laces start

as ivy fingers clutching through

Its crevices

Audiart, Audiart

Stately, tall and lovely tender

Who shall render

Audiart, Audiart

23

Praises meet unto thy fashion?

Here a word kiss

They become freer in *Cathay*, and admirably adapted to the mood of the poems. He achieves a beautifully sustained quality in the following from "The River Song:"

The eastern wind brings the green color into the island

grasses at Yei-shu,

The purple house and the crimson are full of Spring softness.

South of the pond the willow-tips are half-blue and bluer,

Their cords tangle in mist, against the brocade-like palace.

When, however, he seeks greater directness, the rhythms are spare.

At fifteen I stopped scowling,

I desired my dust to be mingled with yours

Forever and forever and forever

Why should I climb the look out?

24

He achieves a remarkable sense of objectivity and absence of sentiment in the various sections of "Mauberley." It would be useless to attempt to describe them in the usual prosodic terms, so inaccurate at best. Here are three examples:

For three years, out of key with his time,

He strove to resuscitate the dead art

Of poetry; to maintain "the sublime"

In the old sense. Wrong from the start.

The lack of strong regular stress is more clearly indicated in the following:

The age demanded an image

Of its accelerated grimace,

Something for the modern stage,

Not, at any rate, an Attic grace.

The sense of loss permeates the following:

Farm's flesh is not to us,

Nor the saints' vision.

25

We have the press for wafer;

Franchise for circumcision.

One short illustration from *Homage to Sextus Propertius* will illustrate his treatment of the long line:

Yet the companions of the Muses

will keep their collective nose in my books,

And weary with historical data, they will turn to my

dance tune.

It would be futile to attempt to give in one illustration from *The Cantos* any conception of the richness of their rhythms. They vary from such definitely poetic ones as the following to those that are flatly prose:

So that the vines burst from my fingers

And the bees weighted with pollen

Move heavily in the vine shoots:

(*XVII*)

Although much of Mr. Pound's verse may be called *free verse*, it does not, in his shorter works, at least, have the loose-

26

ness, or lack of rhythmical construction and intensity that he found in the metres of the new school; nor is the texture achieved by inorganic decoration, or what he called "bill-poster or fence-wash." He sought to, and did, avoid vague words, to weld the "word and thing," and was not afraid of hard statement. The directness of the following is moving:

> Died some, pro patria,
> non "dulce" non "et decor" ...
> walked eye-deep in hell
> believing in old men's lies, then unbelieving
> came home, home to a lie,
> home to many deceits,
> home to old lies and new infamy;
> usury age-old and age-thick
> and liars in public places.

Often, however, he achieves the utmost concentration in single lines like, "His true Penelope was Flaubert," in the portraits of "Brennbaum" and "Mr. Nixon," or most effectively in "The Age Demanded." In these shorter works the form is masterly. His practice accords with his theories.

Mr. Pound's claim to consideration as a major poet must depend, however, on the success or failure of *The Cantos*, and of those it is now time to speak. The theme is, as Mr. Pound said, the tale of a tribe and the effect thereon of usura, a rather vague term as he has used it. Critical opinion on *The Cantos* has been sharply divided. To me, the work is a failure. The reasons are largely structural and technical, but even in subject it is deficient. It was to be "the tale of a tribe," particularly an assault against *usura* as a practice contrary to nature. Aware of the dissolution of the values in the separate segments of modern society, the poet by examining other civilizations—those from which he drew his material for his earlier poems—has sought to discover what has been lost, and out of this gathered knowledge to construct new systems, particularly those which would not permit

27

the various monetary systems that are current. Mr. Pound's difficulty is not that he has chosen civilizations with which even a cultivated reader may be little familiar. Familiarity is not an essential. The modern reader, for example, needs little recourse to footnotes to understand and appreciate the power of Milton's vision in Books XI and XII of *Paradise Lost* when Adam is presented with the pageant of what is to come. Mr. Pound's difficulty is that he has not synthesized his subject and sufficiently transmuted it by his imagination into something vital to the reader.

Some of Mr. Pound's disciples have attempted to defend the economic theories that seemingly motivate *The Cantos*, but with little success. Others have tried to elucidate the subject matter. The interested reader will find the essays by John Drummond, Charles Madge, D. S. Carne-Ross, and G. S. Fraser in· *An Examination of Ezra Pound* particularly valuable for a better understanding of the subject matter of the work. Even their analyses, however, fail to clarify a work that after two complete and many partial readings remains formless, confused, and devoid of a strong impact. Mr. Pound has been especially interested, as Mr. Drummond tells us, "in the point at which an art, or a new phase in the history of an art, springs into life. . . . [He also] maintains that decadence in art, obscurantism in literature, sterility in nature, and injustice in economics, are all symptoms of the same malady." Many persons, however, would not associate the period of Raphael and Michelangelo with decay although the Medicis were powerful exponents of *usura* at the time. I feel about *The Cantos* as Jeffrey did about *The Excursion*: "This will never do." Some critics have called the poem an epic, but if so, the term has been given a new meaning different from that normally associated with the term. From the publication of the earliest cantos the charge of obscurity has been brought against the poem; with the publication of the eighty-fourth the charge is in no danger of disappearing in spite of the attempts by many disciples and admirers of Pound to elucidate the poem. The obscurity arises not so much from the

28

unfamiliarity of the episodes or anecdotes that he relates as from the formlessness of the work as a whole. Mr. Allen Tate has said that there is no other poetry in England "quite so simple in form." He then proceeds to say that the form is "conversation." "*The Cantos* are talk, talk, talk; not by anyone in particular to anyone else in particular; they are just rambling talk. . . . There are . . . three subjects of conversation—ancient times, Renaissance Italy, and the present—but these are not what *The Cantos* are about. They are not about Italy, nor about Greece, nor are they about us. They are not about anything. But they are distinguished verse." Could words say less? Could irresponsibility on the part of a critic be greater? It is such statements—accepted by the unwary as having content—that have often caused modern criticism to be held in disrepute. Since when has any conversation ever had form in the meaning in which we apply the term to a work of art to indicate the careful relationship of the parts? In painting to the integration of line, colour, mass; in poetry to thought, imagery, diction? Mr. Yeats attempted to explain the form in musical terms —that of the fugue. But as Mr. Pound remarked, Yeats didn't know the difference between a fugue and a frog. Incidentally, Mr. Williams thinks Mr. Pound's ear for *tone* little better.

Mr. Pound intended the first eleven cantos to be a preparation of the palette. "I have to get down all the colours or elements I want for the poem," he wrote. "Some perhaps too enigmatically and abbreviatedly. I hope, Heaven help me, to bring them into some sort of design and architecture later." I think he was concerned about the obscurity that confronted the reader. As he wrote to Professor Schelling, "I have managed to make certain passages intelligible in themselves, even though the whole is still unintelligible? ? ? ? Or perhaps I haven't." Later (1927), he confessed to his father, who had questioned him as to the meaning of *The Cantos*, that he was "afraid the whole darn poem is rather obscure, especially in fragments," and he proceeded to outline the main scheme.

29

"1. Rather like, or unlike subject and response and counter subject in fugue.

"A.A. Live man goes down into the world of dead
C.B. The 'repeat in history'
B.C. The 'magic moment' or moment of meta-morphosis, bust through from quotidien into 'divine or permanent world.' Gods, etc.

In Canto XX . . . Nicolo d'Este in sort of delirium after execution of Parasina and Ugo . . .

> *And the Marchese*
> *was nearly off his head*
> *after it all.*

"Various things keep cropping up in the poem. The original world of the gods; the Trojan War, Helen on the wall of Troy with the old men fed up with the whole show and suggesting she be sent back to Greece.

"Rome founded by survivors of Troy. Here ref. to leg-endary founding of Este (condit (founded) *Atesten*, Este.)

"Then in the delirium, Nicolo remembers or thinks he is watching death of Roland. Elvira on wall of Toro (sub-ject-rhyme with Helen on Wall). Epipurgos (on wall); *peur de las hasle* (afraid of sunburn); Neestro (translated in text : let her go back); *ho bios* (life); *cosi Elena vivi* (thus say I Helen, misquote of Dante).

"The whole reminiscence jumbled or 'candied' in Nicolo's delirium. Take that as a sort of bounding surface from which one gives the main subject of the Canto, the lotophagori : lotus eaters, or respectable dope smokers; and general paradiso. You have had hell in Canti XIV, XV; purgatorio in XVI, etc."

There is more in the letter but I think the foregoing gives an accurate idea of what the reader must be prepared for throughout the poem. By 1939, however, writing to Hubert Creekmore as to the form of *The Cantos*, he still was unable to explain himself more clearly than he had already done: "All I can say or pray is: *wait* till it's there. I mean wait till I get 'em written and then if it don't show, I will start exegesis. I haven't an Aquinas-map; Aquinas *not* valid now." In this lies a clue to the great structural weakness of *The Cantos*. The subject of Hell, Purgatory, and Paradise was a fit subject for Dante just because there was a map, and the poet knew when he began where he expected to end—with the beatific vision. The subject of Man's Fall as the result of his disobedience was a fit subject for Milton because he knew in advance the point at which he would arrive—Adam and Eve's expulsion from Eden. The myths were alive and vital. Mr. Pound should have eschewed any myth that had lost its validity, because, by failing to do so, he was prevented from achieving the effect of a cumulative æsthetic intensity that is a prime characteristic of every great epic.

Because of this failure in vision *The Cantos* show a steady disintegration as they proceed. Canto I begins beautifully, and, except for the difficulty arising from obscurity of reference, it is clear. There are beautiful sections in almost every canto of the early ones and the opening of XVII is particularly so. Trouble begins, however, in Cantos XVIII and XIX where the material is that of prose and could not under any circumstances be interesting. After the first thirty cantos the poetic power is less sustained, and reaches the nadir in LII-LXI, those narrating the history of China, and LXII-LXXI, those dealing with John Adams. Since these blocks are a more detailed treatment of material already introduced in the earlier cantos, the reader would expect their poetic intensity to be greater. Actually, I know nothing duller, nothing more prosy and pedestrian. In comparison, Wordsworth's *Excursion* is a work of sustained excitement and sublimity. In the *Pisan Cantos* there is a more personal note, and some critics profess to see in these the beginning of Mr. Pound's resolution of his theme which will lead to the final cantos which will give the desired unity to the work. This, I cannot help thinking, is wishful thinking on their part.

If the form is as defective as I think it is, the beauty of parts can never redeem the whole. Since there is no plot, no psychological analysis, no spiritual struggle, no historical unity— only episodes, and these episodes whether important or trivial bound together only by language, the poet is confronted with a tremendous task of compensating for what he has eschewed. And Mr. Pound fails to compensate.

Mr. Kenner has said that Mr. Pound's principal achievement was the discovery of ways of "making his materials co-exist: classical myths, Christian virtues, Confucian insights, violence and contemplation, casual anecdotes, historical example, Stalin and Arthur Symons get into one poem without mutual devaluation." But is this free association of ideas necessarily a virtue if the reason for this juxtaposition is not readily apparent, particularly since so much of the ground over which he ranges is unfamiliar to most of us? A further difficulty imposed on the reader by one of the poet's chief stylistic devices is his extensive use of ellipsis, closely bound up with this matter of free association. In fact this free association is ellipsis in its larger aspect. The reader is expected to make the leap from one civilization to another—from the Greek to Latin to Provençal to the modern and in any order Mr. Pound sees fit—and to grasp the reason for the juxtaposition. In a smaller aspect it may be entirely personal. Canto LXXIV, the first of the Pisan Cantos, well illustrates his techniques. I choose the following passage because I remember distinctly a similar instance at Marrakech rather than at Tangier:

> but in Tangier I saw from dead straw ignition
> From a snake bite
> fire came to the straw
> from the fakir blowing
> foul straw and an arm-long snake
> that bit the tongue of the fakir making small holes
> and from the blood of the holes
> came fire when he stuffed straw into his mouth

dirty straw that he took from the roadway
first smoke and then the dull flame

So far this is accurate reporting, but completely devoid of the stuff of poetry. But, then, as if it made any difference, Mr. Pound tries to date this incident:

that wd/ have been in the time of Rais Uli
when I rode out to Elson's
near the villa of Perdicaris
or four years before that

Then we encounter a series of ellipses:

elemental he thought the souls of children, if any,
but had rented a shelter for travellers
by foot from Siria, some of them
nor is it for nothing that chrysalids mate in the air
color di luce
green splendour and as the sun thru pale fingers
Lordly men are to earth o'ergiven
these the companions:

In his earlier work Mr. Pound had occasionally used ellipsis, but with none of the frequency we find in *The Cantos*.

Mr. Pound also showed early tendencies toward the polyglot. From a perhaps pardonable mannerism in a young poet anxious to show his erudition this tendency grew to a disease, until, particularly in the later *Cantos*, this polyglot character of his writing is inexcusable. It reveals weakness rather than strength, smallness rather than greatness.

Mr. Pound defended his use of Greek by hoping that it would make some readers study the language. Isn't this sheer conceit on his part? Others have explained his use of foreign languages as his New England conscience preventing his saying in English some of the things, for example, that he said in Latin.

The greatest defect of *The Cantos*, however, lies beyond the bounds of mere technique and is inherent in the poet. His inspiration stems from literature not life. The poet was not only rootless as a person but from the point of view of his culture. It is not only that he expatriated himself, a fact that he has tried to deny, but that he tore himself from the culture that might have fed him and tried to substitute something which starved him rather than gave him nourishment. His letters attest this all too poignantly. Like many, he erred in thinking that a wide knowledge of literature or of the humane studies constitutes a culture. In spite of his miscellaneous erudition, loud rather than deep, the letters reveal a surprisingly sophomoric attitude toward life in general. They reveal the lack of a great and comprehensive soul, of an imagination capable of fusing diverse materials into a great organic unity, of a view of life derived from intimate and at times even grubbing contact with the soil. His attitude was too much determined by literature and particularly literature not always of the first class. We must not deny him his service to American letters, a service manifested in his help to others as well as in his own positive contribution to poetry. We can only regret that, because of circumstances, that service was not greater.

Elinor Wylie
1885—1928

MISS ELINOR WYLIE has been favoured with
a good "press" and she has often been spoken of as one of
America's great women poets. It will be apparent from the following pages that, although I can admire some fifteen of her
poems, I do not think Time will continue to do what her late
husband and his and her friends with ready access to the public's
ear were so able to do for her. The poems on which her reputation will rest are early as well as late, serious, humorous, and
ironic, and are confined to no one subject. Taken in order from
her *Collected Poems*, they are "Velvet Shoes," "Let No
Charitable Hope," "Cold-Blooded Creatures," "Love Song,"
"The little beauty that I was allowed," "I have believed that I
prefer to live," "Little Elegy," "Pretty Words," "Viennese
Waltz," "Golden Bough," and "A Tear for Cressid." Not all
of these are of the same quality and I think none of them ranks
with the truly great lyrics in our heritage of English literature,
and only two with the best of the lyrics of many of the other
poets in this volume.

Miss Wylie has written several autobiographic poems. Two
of them—"Portrait in Black Paint, With a Very Sparing Use
of Whitewash" and "How Many Faults"—published post-
humously by her husband, add details not found in "Wild
Peaches," "Let No Charitable Hope," "Self-Portrait," and "The
little sum of my experience." Essentially a Puritan with a deep
and passionate love of the "austere, immaculate" New England
landscape and with a blood "that owns bare hills, cold silver on
a sky of slate," where spring is "briefer than apple-blossom's
breath," she has a tendency to over-emphasize her state:

35

> *I am, being woman, hard beset;*
> *I live by squeezing from a stone*
> *The little nourishment I get.*
> —"Let No Charitable Hope."

Particularly is she apt to overstress her ability to make a synthesis out of refractory materials and to over-estimate the precision of her mind.

Death is important in her poetry, particularly as a release of the soul from the prison of the body, a release often intimately bound up with love. But it is her treatment of love that will most appeal to the majority of her readers. Her approach is what Mr. Ransom calls the "heart's desire" approach, and it reaches its greatest intensity in the sonnet sequence from Section One of *Angels and Earthly Creatures*, known as "One Person." Although the reader will not question the intensity of the emotion, he may well question the artistry with which she expresses that emotion. At no time is the precision of her mind more open to question than in her treatment of details. Extravagance and confusion are often present. In "The Coast Guard's Cottage" love becomes macabre. Personally, I have always found it difficult to understand why lovers could not be friends, but Miss Wylie, being extremely feminine in her whole approach to life, believes that it is impossible, and is explicit on the subject on several occasions. Her love poems, in spite of their imperfections (or because of them) will appeal to the same readers as does Elizabeth Barrett Browning's "How do I love thee," for which I have never greatly cared.

Miss Wylie has written many poems of pure fancy, a few ballads, and has made some excellent translations. Among these latter, "On a Singing Girl," "To Claudia Homonœa," and "The Lover" have great beauty.

Certain weaknesses of Miss Wylie are obvious; others call for attention. Quite obvious, for example, is the fact that she is incapable of sustained flight. In "Miranda's Supper," she not only fails with the poem as a whole, but the rhyme word often dictates the thought and some of the rhymes are inexcusable. Even in a shorter poem, such as "Wild Peaches," the thought is often dictated by the rhyme rather than the reverse, as, quite obviously, it should be. Bad rhymes occur frequently throughout her poetry. She shows less than the craftsman's care when she rhymes quarters = parterres (131), Nowell (Noël) = trowel (131), centrifugal = unequivocal (162), softly stir = seawater (194-5), clothing = nothing, and parent = errand (206). She shows Emily Dickinson's disregard for them in haunches = inches (212), and breathing = nothing (213). Were not all the other rhymes perfect in the poems in which the foregoing occur, I should say nothing of her deviation, but assume that it was premeditated.

At times Miss Wylie's rhythms, never anything but traditional, are too facile, as in "Silver Filigree" and some of her octosyllabics, always a dangerous measure.

My greatest quarrel is with the details of many of the poems. As pleasant as is "Velvet Shoes," for example, I find "White as a white cow's milk" a little silly. I never thought the whiteness of the cow affected the colour of the milk. In "Sequence," which I confess I find confusing in general, I think her statement that a man might find her skeleton and bury it to "circumvent the wolf" attributes to the wolf an interest in dry bones that he probably does not possess. Were these, too, isolated cases, I should not call attention to them, but such weaknesses flaw poem after poem.

At her best, her images are often excellent. I have already quoted her description of an upper New England spring. Accurate, too, is her picture of the autumn leaves: "The dead leaves are varnished/With colour like blood," (30). She sees the looks on the faces of the passengers as "dull like pebbles, sharp like knives," (18). Some of her best are in "Pretty Words" (240). More conventional are the "sorrowful faces worn/As stone with rain," and occasionally she is trite: "The air was sweeter/Than honey and cream" (134). Too often, however, I find the images inexact. "In coldest crucibles of pain/Her shrinking flesh was fired" (51) says the poet. How does one "fire" in coldest cru-

37

cibles? In the same poem she says that "Pain left her lips more clear than glass;/It coloured and cooled her hand." Isn't the image confused? When in "Pity Me" (85) she asks us to "Pity the wolves who prowl unsleepingly/Guarding the pasture from a thief," isn't she rather careless in her choice of guards? "Now that your eyes are shut," she says in the poem of the same name (93), "Not even a dusty butterfly may brush them." Could it, if the eyes were open? I find equally inexact figures in "Song" (52), "Miranda's Supper" (129 and 131), "Unwilling Admission" (154), "False Prophet" (what, for example, does "silver-curved" mean in "two feathers sprung/Like crescents silver-curved from either temple"?) (155). Is the image clear when she speaks of the "subterranean granite" cloven "to rainbows of the rock's division"? (162). She becomes somewhat involved, too, when she speaks of the attendant spirit guarding her as "in likeness not a lion but a pard" (to rhyme with "hard"), and a few lines later this "pard" has become an archangel.

One image that frequently appears is frankly puzzling. That she repeats it indicates that it must have meant something to her that it fails to mean to me. It first appears in an understandable guise in "Epitaph": "For this she starred her eyes with salt." That could mean, of course, that she wept and her eyes seemed brighter through her tears. In "Sequence (II)," the man will find her skeleton "with stars for eyes, and portent of a sun/Rising between the ribs to frighten him." But in "One Person (X)," she says, after speaking of his sable-silvered hair, "and deep within those caverns are/Your eyesockets, a double-imaged star." Just what is she trying to say in each of the foregoing?

I mentioned that the "heart's-desire" emotion is at its most intense in "One Person," and suggested that the artistry in these sonnets was often questionable. Accepting the extravagance of the emotion, the first ten, except for the details I have mentioned, move forward in a workmanlike manner. Number eleven does not hang together. The last three lines, for example, are confusing. Number twelve develops the mistress-mother idea. In thirteen and fourteen the emotion gets out of control and the result is unfortunate. Fifteen and sixteen continue the theme of self-effacement, which reaches a climax of metaphorical extravagance in seventeen. The person who likes to lose himself in emotion will enjoy the sequence. Another will turn to a more restrained lyric of Mr. Ransom or, if he wishes to know more about modern women poets, will turn to the more detached and beautifully exact lyrics of Miss Moore.

It would be unfair to Miss Wylie, however, not to make some amends. I should like to quote "Viennese Waltz," which captures some of her attitude toward death, sadness, and love, without too much of the extravagance:

We are so tired, and perhaps tomorrow
Will never come; be fugitive awhile
From tears, and let the dancing drink your sorrow
As it has drunk the colour of your smile.

Your face is like a mournful pearl, my darling;
Go, set a rose of rouge upon its white,
And stop your ears against the tiger-snarling
Where lightning stripes the thunder of the night.

Now falling, falling, feather after feather,
The music spreads a softness on the ground;
Now for an instant we are held together
Hidden within a swinging mist of sound.

Forget these frustrate and unhappy lovers;
Forget that he is sad and she is pale;
Come, let us dream the little death that hovers
Pensive as heaven in a cloudy veil.

The extreme simplicity of "Little Elegy" is for me far more effective than her more aureate attempts:

Withouten you
No rose can grow;
No leaf be green
If never seen
Your sweetest face;
No bird have grace
Or power to sing;
Or anything
Be kind, or fair,
And you nowhere.

This and "Velvet Shoes" will certainly be long remembered. In these two the rhythms are more distinctively her own. Elsewhere the music is strongly derivative. There are obvious echoes of Shakespeare, Shelley, and Keats, with an occasional echo of A. E. Housman and Emily Dickinson. Because her rhythms exact no effort from the reader before her music can be enjoyed —it being obvious rather than subtle and delicately modulated— she must pay the penalty of being sooner passed by. Max Friedlander, the great art critic, has remarked that a truly great work will repel before it begins to attract. I have already stated that to be the case with the poetry of Mr. Williams and shall allude to it again in speaking of Mr. Ransom, Miss Moore, and others. Miss Wylie's poetry begins by attracting.

Marianne Moore
1887—

P OETS, says Miss Moore, must be "literalists of the imagination" and must present to the reader for inspection "imaginary gardens with real toads in them." This is an accurate description of her work. The present essay must, therefore, do little more than to provide the commentary for these statements. Miss Moore is a fastidious critic of her own work and has not hesitated to suppress poems that failed to meet her standards. Forty of the forty-eight poems in *Selected Poems* (1935) were chosen from the fifty-four of *Observations* (1925). Of the forty-eight in *Selected Poems* three were deleted in the *Collected Poems*, and of the sixteen in *What Are Years?* (1941), five were deleted from the same volume. Since Miss Moore is not a prolific writer, what were the reasons for her reduction of an already small output?

In almost every instance she has deleted poems in which her personal feelings interfered with her objectivity as an artist. She has a keen satiric humour, and if she wished she could wither a person with her sarcasm. She has preferred the way of strength and removed those poems that show her less than objective. Or, if she has not removed them she has watered the titles, as "My Apish Cousin" reprinted as "The Monkeys." Because she is objective, however, one must not suspect her of a lack of deep feeling. The reader who does not mistake decorum for coldness, elegance for foppishness, and who is sensitive to nuance will be as aware of it as if she had blazoned it forth. A subtle deepening of tone is apparent in each successive volume, finding its most obvious statement in such poems as "In Distrust of Merits," "Keeping Their World Large" and elsewhere.

Because women poets have tended to give love a dominant place in their poetry, Miss Moore's fastidiousness leads her to the opposite extreme. She said what she had to say in "Marriage" (*Observations*), but never reprinted it. Her only other statement is "Efforts of Affection," first printed in *Collected Poems*. Truly, she says,

> . . . *as the sun*
> *can rot or mend, love can make one*
> *bestial or make a beast a man.*

And "efforts of affection attain integration too tough for infraction." Truth in a more concentrated form would be difficult to find.

Her choice of titles reminds one of Mr. Wallace Stevens' practice, although hers seem more pertinent. In many cases they are an integral part of the poem. The title "The Monkeys," for example, is subject of the verb which opens the poem, "winked too much and were afraid of snakes," or "Half Deity" is necessary to the opening "half worm" to describe man.

Her subject matter is largely descriptive of animals, birds, and fish often unfamiliar—even fruit. There are the jerboa, plummet basilisk, buffalo, ostrich, monkey, snake, mongoose, skunk, cat, pelican, pangolins, sea unicorns, snails, octopi—and plums. Many of the things she describes she knows only from pictures or from scientific accounts. Her own perceptivity has been sharpened by the naturalists she has studied. But when she describes gulls no phase of their activity remains unobserved. Except occasionally, she avoids the usual abstractions of death, virtue, courage, love, God, and so forth, that are so frequent a subject matter for poetry and their treatment the test of a poet's worth. She is artist enough to know that it is not the importance of the subject in itself but the skill with which that subject is given significance through form that counts. The heroic paintings of the nineteenth century lack the integrity of the unheroic paintings of the North German school of an earlier age.

Her poems are of "hammered gold and gold enamelling," and nowhere is the enamelling so delicately wrought as in her epithets. Unless it is Hopkins, I know of no modern poet who has sought so assiduously for the right words to depict an object or one who succeeds so well. It is not the single word that she strives for, but all the words necessary for completeness—for the real toads in the garden. Nor does the reader suspect that the effect is spontaneous. The words fall in place with seeming effortlessness, but it is the effortlessness that results from a patient, painstaking, perceptive mind that can fuse diverse materials. And only Miss Moore's notes reveal how diverse that material is. Her eye for detail is evident in her description of the "diffident little newt/with white pin-dots on black horizontal spaced/out bands," and in that of the swan "with flamingo coloured, maple/leaflike feet."

She is particularly sensitive to colour. A sea "the purple of the peacock's neck is/paled to greenish azure." And she speaks of wading "through black jade/of the crow-blue mussel shells. The following simile, clear but concentrated, is highly evocative:

> *from water etched*
> *with waves as formal as the scales*
> *on a fish.*

She speaks, too, of the "backgammon-board wedges interlacing on the wing," of "a moth, almost an owl."

The care expended on her epithets is often apparent in her extensive use of alliteration. On *s*, for example, in the description of the sun finding out the barnacles on the side of the waves:

> *for the submerged shafts of the*
> *sun,*
> *split like spun*
> *glass, move themselves with spotlight swiftness*
> *into the crevices—*
>
> —"The Fish."

43

Or on *b*, in "Abundance":

> *and on the back,*
> *buffy-brown like the breast of the fawn-breasted*
> *bower-bird. It hops like the fawn-breast . . .*

And again on *b* in "Camellia Sabina":

> *the screw-top for this graft-grown*
> *briar-black bloom on black thorn pigeon's blood.*

In her earlier poems, alliteration struck me as being her one concession to traditional poetry.

The reader is constantly delighted with the vividness of her descriptions. When she speaks, for example, of the butterfly with its "apostrophe-tipped brown antennæ porcupining out" or of its "tobacco-brown unglazed china eyes" we feel that "apostrophe," "porcupining," and "china" are perfect.

I think future generations of critics will look back upon the breaking of the dominance of the iambic as one of the greatest contributions to prosody of the early twentieth century. Miss Moore has had a part in this. In her early poems, particularly those she later rejected, the rhythms differed little if at all from those of sensitive prose. As the result of greater experimentation with a technique that is uniquely her own, she has achieved a confidence that has enabled her to communicate a more definite pattern of rhythm without loss of the delicate aloofness than was at first within her powers. It is quite possible that this greater surety is at least partially responsible for the sense of deepening tone that I have mentioned. To express it differently, one could say that the mastery of her technique has enabled her to write on subjects that move her more profoundly than did some of her earlier subjects and still to maintain her attitude of detachment. She is scrupulous in acknowledging her sources, and, because she is so, the reader can see how she has been able to fit others' rhythms into her own pattern. Her stanza patterns

are a valuable aid to her. I had written that although she uses
many patterns, her best work is generally found in those few
which she has most frequently used. When I returned to the
poems for verification, however, I realized I had made too easy
a generalization. In one poem, "Elephants," she uses an a-b-a-b
stanza pattern in which her stronger than usual but still flexible
rhythms reflect the massiveness of the subjects. Ordinarily,
however, she makes extensive use in her stanza pattern of assonance and consonance. The most distinctive characteristic of
her verse patterns is her use of what has been called light-rhyme
and the way in which the stanzas are interdependent. The last
three stanzas of "The Fish" illustrate what I mean.

> *All*
> *external*
> > *marks of abuse are present on this*
> > *defiant edifice—*
> > > *all the physical features of*
>
> *ac-*
> *cident—lack*
> > *of cornice, dynamite grooves, burns, and*
> > *hatchet strokes, these things stand*
> > > *out on it; the chasm-side is*
>
> *dead.*
> *Repeated*
> > *evidence has proved that it can live*
> > *on what cannot revive*
> > > *its youth. The sea grows old in it.*

Rhymes like *all*—exter*nal*, *ac-* —*lack*, *dead*—repea*ted* call, of
course, for a slightly different emphasis than they would normally
receive, but they give a feeling of suspension that is heightened
by the conflict at the end of the stanza. The reader stresses the
-ed of "repeated" more than he normally would; he hesitates
slightly at "and" rhyming with "stand," and at "is" and "of"

at the end of the stanzas. Every reader can, of course, find numerous examples of her practice. I think it beautifully exemplified in two later poems, "Half-Deity" and "Virginia Britannia."

Miss Moore's poems are often deceptive in their apparent descriptiveness. The casual reader is apt to miss the general observations that lie beneath the surface of the drama. In her earlier work these were not so carefully integrated in the poem as they later became, although in the later as well as the earlier these are seemingly casually dropped into a descriptive passage. Such statements as "the feigned inconsequence of manner, best bespeak that weapon, self protectiveness," "gesticulation—it is half the language," or "sleep—epitome of what is to him as the average person, the end of life," betray their too self-conscious casualness. In her later poems, however, the various elements of the poem are so carefully integrated that she seems to follow Mr. Frost's rule for writing a poem—to move in a zig-zag fashion directly to your object. "He 'Digesteth Harde Yron' " well illustrates this. She begins with a comparison of the camel-sparrow to the extinct roc and moa, proceeds to the bird's nesting habits, its characteristics and reasons for its being valued—its plumes, its eggs, as a riding-beast—and the symbolic value of the products which

> . . . dramatize a
> meaning always missed
> by the externalist.

> The·power of the visible
> is the invisible; as even where
> no tree of freedom grows,
> so-called brute courage knows.
> Heroism is exhausting, yet
> it contradicts a greed that
> did not wisely spare
> the harmless solitaire

of great auk in its grandeur.
Unsolicitude having swallowed up
all giant birds but an
alert gargantuan
little-winged, magnificently
speedy running-bird. This one
remaining rebel
is the sparrow-camel.

The reader's memory has been stirred, his imagination whetted, and his mind lifted beyond the moment. Interesting, too, is the deceptive manner by which she leads the reader in " 'Keeping the World Large' " from musing about Italy to an attack on our own philistinism:

Keeping their world large, that silent
marching marching marching and this silence
for which there is no description, are

the voices of fighters with no rests between,
who would not yield;
whose spirits and whose bodies
all too literally were our shield, are still our shield,
They fought the enemy, we fight
fat living and self pity. Shine, O shine
unfalsifying sun, on this sick scene.

She reveals her sense of form, too, in "Nevertheless" in the manner in which she leads to and away from her statement: "Victory won't come to me unless I go to it." She displays a keen dramatic sense in "Bird-Witted," the story of the protection from the cat by the mocking-bird of her three babies.

I first became acquainted with Miss Moore's poetry in *The Dial* when poetry—particularly experimental poetry—meant little to me. It was not until preparing for the present volume that I returned to her work. Instead of obscurity I found clarity.

No poet of today is so little obscure as she. It is the eye-appearance of her poems on the page that would disturb the reader unfamiliar with her work. She has more reason for hers than has Mr. Cummings for his. Instead of preciosity I found a highly developed sensitivity to the visual world; instead of coldness and sterility, a shy and reticent aloofness, with a delightful sense of humour. I think Miss Moore performs a highly educative function. At a time when "little we see in nature that is ours" is a too prevalent attitude she has called our attention to minutiæ that make life richer and pleasanter. We must recognize that many of the minutiæ, however, are the results of a fact in a book sprung to life through the vivifying powers of her imagination. She speaks of Ireland, for example, as "the kindest place I've never been" and as "the greenest place I've never seen."

To readers who do not like ceremony, Miss Moore has little to say, because however perceptive, charming, witty—yes, even philosophical—she may happen to be, she places great value on ceremony. She will always serve you tea in porcelain cups, and she will not insist you take lemon, but she may slip a little piece into your cup. She will always provide thin bread and butter with a little jam. You must never, never expect, even when you are most thirsty or hungry, that she will offer you beer and a ham-on-rye. At such times you should drop in on your men friends.

John Crowe Ransom
1888—

From the point of view of *Selected Poems*, Mr. John Crowe Ransom is an "obscure" rather than a "pure" poet. By his own definition of the terms, a "pure" poet is one who "will not consider a subject which lends itself to moralization; that is, a subject of practical interest"; an "obscure" poet is one who "may take the subject nearest his own humanity, a subject perhaps of terrifying import; but in treating it will stop short of all moral or theoretical conclusions, and confuse his detail to the point where it leaves no positive implications." These are useful definitions if not applied too rigidly and will explain many things about his poetry that might otherwise lead to misinterpretation. They will make clear, in part at least, the basis of his choice for *Selected Poems* (1945), but they will fail to include many poems from his earlier volumes.

Mr. Ransom has not been a prolific poet and understandably so. Apart from his professorial and editorial duties, his poetic fastidiousness and his high degree of critical objectivity toward his own poetry would prevent prolixity. Since 1919 he has published only five small volumes of poetry, two of which were selections from the other three. *Grace After Meat*, containing twenty poems, was a selection from the thirty-three in *Poems about God* (1919) and the forty-eight in *Chills and Fever* (1924). Thirty-seven of the forty-two in *Selected Poems* (1945) were a selection from the forty-eight in *Chills and Fever* and fifty in *Two Gentlemen in Bonds* (1927). It is not only interesting but characteristic that this latest volume contains nothing from the first. In other words, almost twenty years after the publication of over one hundred and thirty poems, Mr. Ransom chose only thirty-seven to be included in his final selection; and he has written no new poems in many years. These bare statistics can be of value if rightly understood. What was his basis for exclusion? Why, for example, did he exclude such poems as "Overtures," "November," "Plea in Mitigation," "These Winters," "Little Boy Blue," "Amphibious Crocodile," and others—all poems of merit? No one reason is sufficient to explain his choice, but we can better understand him if, without seeking a definite answer to this question, we at least keep it in mind.

Just as Mr. Frost has approached the universal from the subject matter of New England, so has Mr. Ransom approached it from that of the South. It would be a mistake, however, to think of him as a regional poet. The idiosyncrasies of many sitters for portraits—of Miss Euphemia, the old man of "Nocturne," Brady ("On the Road to Wockensutter"), Mr. Minnit, Miriam Tazewell, Emily Hardcastle, and Grimes ("Puncture")—may have stemmed from his southern background, but they have a universal interest. The love of and sensitivity to nature apparent in "The Sunset," "Antique Harvesters," "Of Margaret," in particular, but with suggestions of it everywhere, is the love that springs from an intimate knowledge of the South—a knowledge, however, that is unnecessary on the part of the reader for an appreciation of its influence on Mr. Ransom.

The things that have absorbed him are those that have always absorbed the attention of poets: God, death, love, childhood, age, and other universals. His treatment, however, chiefly differs from the more customary treatment in his seeming objectivity. The reader should not be deluded by the poet's unobtrusive insistence on decorum. He is aloof rather than cold; reticent and shy rather than disinterested. He prefers not to reveal his sensitivity and tenderness to one less sensitive than he. Irony and humour are a cloak to, rather than a substitute for, his passion. We could even say that they are in equipoise. The probability of the years having intensified this reluctance to self-revelation is perhaps the reason for the suppression of many early poems of greater frankness. These, only infrequently bordering on the sentimental, are rightly to be distrusted. The true aristocrat, fully aware of his kinship with the poet, will participate in an emotion that remains undisclosed to vulgar eyes. It is the emotion in the music of Mozart and Schubert, rather than that in Tschaikowsky, Wagner, or Brahms. To achieve this result, Mr. Ransom depends not so much on understatement as on his subtle manipulation of his rhythms, on his diction, images, and allusions—matters for later discussion.

The subject of God is chiefly found in *Poems about God*, an unfortunate title. The poems would repel the pious attracted by the title, and would fail to attract those who would be sympathetic. Many of these poems are humorous and ironic and reflect the thinking of every inquiring, healthy youth. Hardy-like are the questions he poses in "Geometry," and "The Cloak Model." He reveals a sincere social consciousness in "The Power of God." The weakness of these poems about God, however, is the weakness of expression rather than of idea. The rhythms are in the Georgian tradition and lack the tautness of his later work. They are too smooth, and no one knows better than Mr. Ransom that it is easy for a technician to write smooth metres. He had still to learn the technique of a modern poet, that, as he himself says, "of going over [his work] laboriously and roughening it." He approaches the rougher rhythms in "Prayer," a sharply ironic poem that would offend the pious, but does not wholly succeed until in later work. He develops them in "Night Voices," and fulfils his aim in "Our Two Worthies," a plea for unity in religion. In this irony-free poem about Jesus the Paraclete and Paul the Exegete, he approaches his ideal of anonymity by keeping the passion under strict control with a four-stress couplet that is light and dry.

More interesting than his treatment of God is his treatment of love. The early poems on this subject, none of which he has reprinted, alert the reader to its treatment in the later poems. In these earlier ones he is less objective, less reticent than he later became. All of them reveal that he looks on poetry not as an escape, but as a means to a greater reality. "The Sunset," "The

Lover," "Overtures" are less anonymous in their treatment and more apparent in their emotion than "Winter Remembered," "April Treason," and others. It is the more anonymous poems on love, however, that reveal his greater power. He is not concerned with that aspect of love which interests itself in wish-fulfilment, or what he has called "heart's-desire" poetry. He is fascinated, as was Hardy, by the obstacles to completeness. Whether that obstacle was God ("The Sunset"), the fear of ridicule ("The Lover"), a quarrel ("Overtures"), a misconception ("Spectral Lovers"), or absence ("Winter Remembered," "Jack's Letter") makes little difference. He dwells, too, on the bitter realization that a young idealist often encounters after marriage —that the person he has won is soulless ("Triumph," "Two Sonnets"), or unaware of the responsibilities of marriage ("Husband Betrayed"), and realizes that an absorption in his beloved blinds him to things he would otherwise appreciate ("Spring Posy"). Mr. Ransom has chosen for inclusion in *Selected Poems* only those love poems that are almost completely anonymous such as "Parting at Dawn," "Vaunting Oak," "Parting, Without a Sequel," "Two in August," "Somewhere is Such a Kingdom," "The Equilibrists," and others. More restrained than the earlier ones, either by understatement, by the lightening of the rhythms, or by a deft humour, the careful reader will nevertheless grasp their emotion.

When the passion is intensely personal, even those devices cannot conceal the fire beneath an urbane exterior and attempted objectivity. Several poems, essentially autobiographic, give a keen insight into the poet's nature. Some of the love poems, it is true, have a personal ring, but it is not such poems as "Miller's Daughter," or "Hilda" or any of the aforementioned ones that I mean. It is rather such poems as "Tom, Tom, the Piper's Son," "Plea in Mitigation," "These Winters" (indicating as they do loneliness, misunderstanding, regret over the less-heroic present), "November," "Prometheus in Straits," "Morning," "Antique Harvesters," and others, that make the reader incisively aware of the poet's deeply passionate nature.

Two poems, "The Swimmer" and "Persistent Explorer," reflect a different facet of this nature—the presence and mastery of the death-wish, in both cases death by water, reminiscent with a difference of Mr. Frost's "The Leaf-Treader." It is only natural that the poet's high idealism should occasionally be outraged by spiritual aridity. He has admiration for the "manliness of men" as exhibited by the average man who will face danger or calm, keeping his blue eyes blue to any weather ("Men," "Wrestling") but he recognizes that some men are incapable of a full life ("Men without Sense of Direction"). In this he is a true democrat; but he is also disturbed by the failure of men to utilize their gifts and deplores the crass materialism of many of his compatriots ("Prometheus in Straits," "Amphibious Crocodile," "Philomena"). His deeply religious nature is best glimpsed in his seemingly casual allusions.

He is frequently at his best in his poems about children. He is interested in their active imaginations and their absorption in their own world ("First Travels of Max," "Janet Waking"). He is aware of their cruelty ("In Mr. Minnit's House"), but he can sympathize with the grandfather who preferred to play with the children rather than to be bored with the materialism of the adults ("Old Man Playing with Children"). His two most moving poems on children are, however, those about children taken by death, the one a charming little girl and the other a rather nasty boy ("Bells for John Whiteside's Daughter," "Dead Boy"). Since it is the poet's deft treatment that raises them above other poems on childhood, consideration of them will be reserved until later.

Except for the pervasive quality of the poet's sensuous awareness to nature in all of its aspects, the other subjects, such as old age, a parent's disillusionment, mental unbalance ("The Vagrant," "Boris of Britain," "Winter's Tale"), and his portraits comprising a noteworthy collection of idiosyncratics receive anonymous treatment and are more cerebral than heartfelt. This is no disparagement of them, because Mr. Ransom is too highly skilled a technician, too keen an observer of significant minutiæ, possessed of a too-highly developed sense of empathy not to be able to invest them with life.

The foregoing exposition of the poet's subject matter does not, of course, aim at completeness, nor does it suggest that the poems selected for illustrative purposes are necessarily the best. Its purpose was to give the reader a clearer idea of the range of his subject matter than is possible from *Selected Poems*. It has neglected, for example, many poems on biblical subjects that belong under several possible headings, as, for example, "Judith of Bethulia" and "Armageddon," or the incident based on St. Bartholomew's Massacre ("Necrological"), or a subject based on a local incident ("Old Mansion") included in *Selected Poems*. Mr. Ransom has revealed his highly developed self-critical faculty by his rejection of many of them.

The only objection of many readers will be to his merciless excisions for his final selection. As I have suggested, however, this is understandable. His reticence, as well as his sense of fastidious elegance, has steadily increased, and, having risen above those annoyances so perplexing in one's younger years, he has too drastically reduced the number of poems by which he wishes to be judged.

More important, of course, than the subject matter for a proper appreciation of the post is his treatment of that subject-matter. Has he carefully integrated his imagery, diction, rhythms, allusions, selection of detail, and transformed the raw subject-materials into works of art capable of producing a strong æsthetic effect?

Mr. Ransom has experimented with numerous stanza forms, often with outstanding success. He has employed *terza rima* (both regular and inverted), irregular forms, stanzas varying from three to seven lines in rhyme (both on the stressed and un-stressed syllable), in assonance, or rhymeless. He has once used Skeltonics. His chief experimentation has been with stanzas of four, five, and six lines, four predominating. His four-line stanzas present a multiplicity of rhymes and stresses. To achieve anything even approaching accurate information about the structure of his lines, however, the investigator soon realizes, as I have repeatedly pointed out, that it is futile to use the highly inaccurate although traditional system of iambs, anapests, trochees, and so forth. That system with its many variations—more often confusing than enlightening—stops short of the point at which an examination of Mr. Ransom's poetry should begin. His stresses, for example, are sometimes heavy, but more often they are so light as to be almost imperceptible. The usual stress mark (′) does not distinguish. Nor does the alternation of ′ with ∪ accurately indicate the time element involved; and it is this subtle indication of time that constitutes one of his most distinguishing characteristics. As I have mentioned, a more accurate notational method—that of Thomson—begins where the old notation ends.

In *Poems about God* the rhythms are predominantly traditional and derivative. "The Swimmers," for example, with each stanza built on a single rhyme, recalls the second half of the stanza of Hardy's "Weathers." Elsewhere there are frequent echoes of Frost. The only suggestion in this poem of the later work is the selection of certain humorous details or sound repetitions; these, however, have not been perfected. In "Wrestling" and "Prayer," both unrhymed poems, we have the first anticipation of a new voice. The poet is striving for speech rhythms that are his own. He is trying to avoid the strong iambic beat that is the bane of so much second- and third-rate poetry and return to the muscular flexibility that is our English tradition from before Chaucer until the latter part of the seventeenth century, when in spite of all that Dryden could do to prevent it, the iamb gained its mastery. Fortunately, it is finally being put in its place. Such lines as

♪ | ♪ | ♪ | ♪. ♪ | ♪ ′ ♪ | ♪ ♪ | ♪. ♪
At last came thresh-ing time, the man-ly seas-on

or "But one was there some twenty miles a stranger," identical with the preceding, anticipates his later line. It is not only such

55

measures as |♪ |♪ that are characteristic, but a device he uses at the end of a line, as in

♪ | ♩ ♪ ♪ ♪♪ | ♩ '♪ | ♪. ♪|♪ ♩
We had a champ-ion there. He looked and list-ened

That is, instead of the stressed syllable receiving the longer time, as is characteristic of a true iamb (♪|♩ ♪|♩), it is the unstressed element that is lengthened, a fact impossible to indicate by the traditional notation. Some readers will prefer a different reading of a measure like *last came* (| ♪. | ♪.), and will wish no accent bar before *came*. That could read|♪ ♪.. It is no longer necessary to say (and I have already confessed my past guilt) that he achieves a contrapuntal effect by superimposing the rhythms of speech on a basic iambic pattern. If not double talk, this is still vague and leaves too much for the reader to interpret. A variation on the foregoing ending occurs in the first line of "Prayer":

♪| ♪. |♪| ♩ ♪| ♩ '♪| ♩ ♪| ♪. ♪
She would not keep at home, the fool-ish wom-an

But let us analyse a few stanzas from the poems in *Selected Poems*. Stanza three of "Winter Remembered" has a distinctive music that is unique with Mr. Ransom, particularly lines two and four:

|♪ ♪ ♪| ♪. | ♩ ♪ ♪| ♪ ♪ ♪|♩
Bet-ter. to walk forth in the murd-er-ous air

♪| ♩ ♪| ♩ ♪ ♪| ♩ ♪ ♪ ♪|♪. ♪
And wash my wound in the snows; that would be heal-ing;

♪| ♩ ♪| ♪. ♪| ♩ ♪| ♩ ♪| ♩
Be-cause my heart would throb less pain-ful there,

|♪.♪ | ♩ ♪| ♩. ♪| ♩ ♪| ♪ ♪ ♪
Be-ing caked with cold, and past the smart of feel-ing.

56

Even more characteristic are the stanzas of "Necrological." Here is the fourth:

Not all were white; some go-ry and fab-u-lous

Whom the sword had pierced and then the grey wolf eat-en;

But the broth-er reas-oned that he-roes' flesh was thus,

Flesh fails, and the pos-tured bones lie weath-er-beat-en.

A stanza from a poem in a different metre will further illustrate how Mr. Ransom has used speech rhythms to achieve the right mood. In "Janet Waking" he has so manipulated the rhythms that he has caught the feeling of an adult toward an incident that is tragic for a child. Rhythm, of course, only partially explains the success of this poem. Here is stanza one:

Beau-ti-ful-ly Jan-et slept

Till it was deep-ly mor-ning. She woke then

And thought a-bout her daint-y-feath-ered hen,

To see how it had kept.

In "Bells for John Whiteside's Daughter," certainly one of his great poems, he keeps the stresses light and the rhythms supple.

His speech rhythms differ from those of other poets in that they are faster paced. As a result they are less earthy and more urbane. They are free, too, of the elegiac quality that often is a characteristic of a poet who seems to be hammering his thoughts

57

into shape as he writes; instead, his have the brilliance of a quick mind whose thoughts are completely crystallized before he speaks. It is the movement of a person who speaks with spontaneous wit. Such a movement, however, is the result of studied concentration and much revision. The lightness is helped, of course, by his selection of vowel sounds in relation to his consonants. He rarely uses heavy vowels or harsh consonants, but makes abundant use of liquids and nasals.

However important to his effects are his rhythms and vowel and consonantal sounds, it is his diction which does much to enhance his seeming objectivity. I am not here speaking of his use of learned or archaic words like "sæculum," "stuprate," "pernoctate," "halidom," "thole," and others, or of such phrases as "aquarelles of ditches" (echoes of Wallace Stevens?), but of words used to understate an emotion. In "Bells for John White-side's Daughter," "astonishes" and "vexed," for example, to describe the attitude toward her death of those who loved the little girl, or of "brown study" (used twice), to describe her as she lay in her coffin, indicate the poet's anti-Romantic tendencies. In the same way that the poet used the three middle stanzas to describe with humour her lively activities when alive in order to divert his mind from the grief of the present moment, so do these words help to convey the conscious effort of the mourners to resist being engulfed by sorrow. His use of "sternly stopped" to describe the effect of the bells on these efforts to remain aloof from their grief enhances it. The poignancy of a fighting self-discipline is at such times more deeply moving and tragic than a visible surrender to the emotions. In "Dead Boy" he is even more daring. Understatement dominates stanza one. In stanzas two and three he uses metaphor to show the unpleasant qualities of the boy while alive—"a black cloud full of storms too hot for keeping," "a sword beneath his mother's heart," "a pig with a pasty face." Stanza four returns to the details of the funeral where the elder men of the family try to conceal their grief. This is an admirable example of the poet's powers of condensation:

The elder men have strode by the box of death
To the wide flag porch, and muttering low they sound
The bruit of day. O friendly waste of breath!
Their hearts are hurt by a deep dynastic wound.

His practice is just the opposite of Mr. Eliot's in his *Four Quartets*. And Mr. Ransom is often a more profound thinker than Mr. Eliot. Whereas he wears his erudition lightly, and tends to conceal his profundity behind a mask of light irony and graceful almost dancing rhythm, Mr. Eliot, by means of heavier rhythms, a magisterial tone (some readers would prefer "penitential"), and an arrangement of suggestive words that sound mystical and profound, gets away with the veriest commonplaces. The sceptical reader can easily test this by reading the *Quartets*, even better by listening to Mr. Eliot's recordings of them.

I am sorry Mr. Ransom has not included "Little Boy Blue" in his *Selected Poems*, because this charming poem, based on the nursery rhyme, and with no greater significance, fills in the details that are lacking in the original. But what details! The charm lies not only in those, but in the deft twists of rhythm and a mixture of words from almost every level, among them "continuum" and "blowzy." His choice of "transmogrifying" as an adjective for the bee that stung Chucky ("Janet Waking") certainly lightens the tragedy of his death and captures the proper tone of the poem. Successful as the poet has been in the majority of cases, I think he just misses in "Here Lies a Lady." The oftener I read the poem the more inclined am I to think so. Technically, it is brilliant, but is it not also heartless?—quite the contrary of "Bells for John Whiteside's Daughter." Were he describing a foolish, shallow woman, the tone would be more nearly appropriate, but, even so, the woman had inspired deep affection. I find, for example, the suggestive quality of the line "In love and great honour we bade God rest her soul" out of keeping with the general tone. The details of two emotions are out of balance.

It is obviously impossible to do more than suggest the poet's use of significant detail as a means of enhancing the total æsthetic effect. Naturally, the efficacy of the detail is closely linked with the accuracy of epithet. "Antique Harvesters," one of his most successful poems because it conveys with such restraint his deep love for his homeland, abounds with examples. Stanza one illustrates the details of epithet:

> *Tawny are the leaves turned but they still hold,*
> *And it is harvest; what shall this land produce?*
> *A meagre hill of kernels, a runnel of juice;*
> *Declension looks from our land, it is old.*
> *Therefore let us assemble, dry, grey, spare,*
> *And mild as yellow air.*

"Tawny" is not only accurate, but imaginative. A northerner unconsciously contrasts it with the more brilliant autumn foliage to which he is accustomed. "Meagre," "kernels," "runnel," and "declension" suggest worn-out soil, but "yellow air" is almost a compensation. On a larger scale is his introduction of the fox hunters:

> *We pluck the spindling ears and gather the corn.*
> *One spot has special yield? "On this spot stood*
> *Heroes and drenched it with their only blood."*
> *And talk meets talk, as echoes from the horn*
> *Of the hunter—echoes are the old man's arts,*
> *Ample are the chambers of their hearts.*

> *Here come the hunters, keepers of a rite;*
> *The horn, the hounds, the lank mares coursing by*
> *Straddled with archetypes of chivalry;*
> *And the fox, lovely ritualist, in flight*
> *Offering his unearthly ghost to quarry;*
> *And the fields, themselves to harry.*

> *Resume, harvesters.*

"*Spindling* ears," "*only* blood," "*lank* mares . . . *straddled* with *archetypes* of chivalry," the fox, the "lovely *ritualist*," the haunting rhythm of "talk meets talk as echoes from the horn/ Of the hunter" and the ellipsis in the repetition of "echoes" for the rich suggestiveness of lines five and six of the stanza—these are but a few of the details that make this a richly rewarding poem.

"Vaunting Oak," "Emily Hardcastle, Spinster," "Good Ships," "Old Mansion," all in fact, of the poems in *Selected Poems* offer treasures to the thoughtful and sensitive reader. He will be amused by the sustained metaphor of "Good Ships," by the delightful suggestiveness of the alliterating "I was dapper when I dangled" of "Emily Hardcastle, Spinster," and moved to admiration by the appropriateness of his similes, and by his subtly introduced allusions, often of great erudition.

Do I have only praise for Mr. Ransom's poetry? Not entirely. Except for one or two poems in *Poems about God*, I think his reputation is enhanced by not reprinting those in that volume. The poems in *Chills and Fever* and *Two Gentlemen in Bonds* are of a much higher technical achievement than any in his first volume and are valuable for the insight they give us of the poet; but, except for a few that I have elsewhere mentioned, he has chosen those best destined for survival. Many of the others are deficient in body. Only a very few of *Selected Poems* leave me untouched. In spite of many readings and with an admiration for most of it, I am puzzled by the ending of "Armageddon." I cannot see his purpose. Nor do "Spiel of the Three Mountebanks" and "Captain Carpenter" strike me as successful in spite of their technical proficiency. From my point of view, they lack significance. But this is a relatively inconsequential matter.

Mr. Ransom is generally spoken of as a minor poet, although one of our best. What do the terms "minor" and "major" mean, if anything, when applied to poets? I prefer not to classify him. He is obviously a poet of exquisite taste, of gentlemanly aloofness, with a highly developed technical competence, a warm, vibrant, sensitive personality kept under admirable restraint, a person of erudition. With every reading these qualities become more apparent in a greater number of poems. Moreover, he has written enough poems of unquestionable merit to indicate that his success was not accidental. Certainly, these are sufficient to place him in the ranks of America's best. The reader who needs judgments from the poet will be disappointed. Mr. Ransom could easily make them, and has often implied them, but we must remember that judgments were foreign to his aim. He preferred to be an "obscure" poet, to "stop short of all moral or theoretical conclusions, and to confuse his detail to the point where it leaves no positive implications." Need we ask more than that he should have admirably succeeded within his self-prescribed limits?

Conrad Aiken
1889—

MR. CONRAD AIKEN has drawn the subject
matter for his poetry from the fields of psychology, psycho-
analysis, philosophy, as well as from his own experience. He
has posed such timeless questions as Who am I and why? What
am I and how? Where am I going? What is the nature of God?
Of the meaning of life? Of death? What is this thing called
love? and others. Certainly, during a period when poetry has
too often concerned itself with minutiæ of petty and frustrated
egos, he cannot be accused of triviality. And whether or not
what he has to say will be of particular interest to the specialists
in his subject matter is of small concern. We are only interested
in whether or not, with various aspects of these themes as a
basis, he has written good poetry.

During a period when many of the younger poets were
experimenting with the traditional rhythms to try to bring
them closer to contemporary speech rhythms, Mr. Aiken experimented in a different way. He set out to see if he could
accomplish in poetry what musicians had accomplished in symphonies, improvisations, themes and variations, preludes, and
other forms.

Mr. Aiken has republished six of his early long poems, three
of them called symphonies, under the title *The Divine Pilgrim*
(1949), and of those let us speak first. The fact that he has
revised these in varying degrees and republished them indicates
that he is content to have them rest on their merits and not be
regarded as early work. The titles with some of Mr. Aiken's
condensed statements about them follow: "The Charnel Rose"

63

[1915] ("needed, and received, severe treatment"), "The Jig of Forslin" [1915-1916] ("little altered"), "The House of Dust" [1916-1917] ("much revised, although not much cut"), "Senlin: A Biography" [1918] ("considerably revised for the Hogarth Press edition in 1925, has now been revised again, in some instances back to the original"), "The Pilgrimage of Festus [1918-1920] ("to all intents unchanged"), "Changing Mind" [1925, published in *John Deth*, 1930] ("the specific 'I' of the artist, or writer, and his predicament, both private and social, as the articulator of man's evolving consciousness").

Aware of the misunderstanding of these six poems on the part of many readers, Mr. Aiken has provided his own programme. A careful reader will find this unnecessary, because the poet states his theme in the poetry itself. But, to quote the poet, the theme of "Charnel Rose" is "nympholepsy . . . that impulse which sends man from one dream, or ideal, to another, always disillusioned, always creating for adoration some new and subtle fiction." That of "The Jig of Forslin" [Forslin meaning "chanceling or weakling"] "is an exploration of his emotional and mental hinterland, his fairyland of impossible illusions and dreams." Of "The House of Dust," "is really an elaborate progressive analogy between the city, seen as a multicellular living organism, and the multicellular or multineural nature of human consciousness. . . . The movement is from physiological to psychological." Of "Senlin: A Biography," [Senlin means "the little old man that each of us must become"] "an extension and analysis of that perennially fascinating problem of personal identity which perplexes each of us all his life: the basic and possibly unanswerable question, *who and what I am*, how is it that I am I, Senlin, and not someone else? . . . For Senlin discovers not only that he is a whole gallery of people or personalities, rather than one, but also that this discovery is as incommunicable as it is elusive." Of "The Pilgrimage of Festus," "a cerebral adventure, of which the motive is a desire for knowledge . . . the possibility [that] knowledge is itself limited: that knowledge is perhaps so conditioned by the conditions of the knower that it can have but little relative value." Of "Changing Mind," "the specific 'I' and a specific moment in its experience, in a specific predicament: the predicament, both private and social, of the writer or artist."

Although the reader does not, as I have said, need Mr. Aiken's programme in order to understand the poem, this is not true of the "The Charnel Rose," the first of the symphonies. Few readers would grasp from reading the poem in its original or revised state that "beginning with the lowest order of love, the merely carnal, the theme leads irregularly, with returns and anticipations as in music, through various phases of romantic or idealistic love, to several variants of erotic mysticism; finally ending in a mysticism apparently pure. . . . The protagonist of the poem is . . . man in general . . . seeking in many ways to satisfy his instinct to love, worshipping one idol after another, disenchanted with each in turn; and at last taking pleasure not so much in anticipation as in memory." The poem is divided into four main sections, and each of these into from three to six sub-sections. The music varies from one to the other, sometimes vague and impressionistic with lines of uneven length and irregular rhyme, sometimes with lines of strong and regular beat rhyming in couplets. The difficulty lies not in a crabbed syntax or conscious obscurities, as with too many younger poets with nothing to say, but in the symbols, because at no time is there overt statement. Nor does the reader feel the inevitability of what is said. The diction tends to the aureate rather than to the exact. We encounter terms like *gold, silver, whirled, swirled,* and other words abounding in liquids and nasals until we become too aware of the essential lack of firmness of texture and of significant form. The attention is apt to wander and lose itself in a welter of lulling sound. We have lines like "Black ripples on the pool chuckled of passions" and "Cold and gold and green-gleamed white" which typify not the rare but the usual lines. The effect is vague, and sheer verbal music is not enough. Mr. Aiken reveals in this poem a defect of many of our modern poets, among whom we can include Mr. Auden. He loves words

65

for their sound alone rather than for the communicative value in which sound plays an important role.

The manner in which Mr. Aiken states his theme can be better illustrated in "The Jig of Forslin":

> *In the mute evening, as the music sounded,*
> *Each voice of it, wearing gold or silver,*
> *Seemed to open a separate door for him . . .*
> *Suave horns eluded him down corridors;*
> *Persuasive violins*
> *Sang of nocturnal sins;*
> *And ever and again came the hoarse clash*
> *Of cymbals; as a voice that swore of murder.*
> *Which way to choose, in all this labyrinth?*
> *Did all lead in to the self same chamber?*
> *No matter: he would go . . .*
> *In the evening, as the music sounded;*
> *Streaming swift and thin, or huddled slow . . .*

At the end of the poem Forslin realizes that his dreams have confused themselves with reality until "he does not know if this is wake or dreaming." Having followed Forslin with growing impatience and boredom, my own reaction is that I could scarcely care less. I have encountered some striking scenes and have experienced some lovely music, often anticipating or echoing that of Mr. Eliot, but for what purpose? I have not been led to greater reality but from it, and escape from life has never held my interest.

The point toward which Mr. Aiken is driving becomes clearer in "The House of Dust." His preface to the poem from which I have already quoted is rather a grandiose statement of the obvious—the process of growing up. In Part III, Section 9, he generalizes on the vicarious experiences of the early part of the poem. The poet has turned inward in order to give meaning to the outward meaninglessness of life. Or, to quote him,

if it has a meaning,
Too tiresomely insistent on one meaning:
Futility . . .

. . . We grope our way a little,
And then grow tired. No matter what we touch,
Dust is the answer—dust: dust everywhere.

The poet realizes, however, that we must all put faith in something. Against this poem I make the same complaint as against "The Jig of Forslin." The verse is too monotonously sweetly musical for sustained interest and the treatment of the material is unnecessarily prolix. The effect is impressionistic rather than incisive, the diction, particularly his epithets, musical rather than exact, the whole lacking in significant form. He has sought to deprive words of their intellectual association and to use them as a means for achieving absolute music—music that is dissociated from a programme. But the fact that he has employed a traditional syntax and an accepted vocabulary makes it impossible for the general reader to go along with him. As a result, instead of having absolute music, he becomes conscious of the overabundance of examples used for the induction at which he arrives. The reader senses luxuriant indulgence rather than economy. Instead, therefore, of achieving the significant form of a Haydn or Mozart symphony he gives us something more nearly akin to the diffuse symphonies of Bruchner and Mahler. He gives us romantic prolixity in its most decadent form rather than the classic restraint of all great art.

In "Senlin: An Autobiography," we find a more varied music than in the earlier works. The texture of the verse is tighter than heretofore, and the poet poses questions the consideration of which transports us from the world of dreams and vicarious experience to the present. The poet alerts the reader to realities about which he may hitherto have been unaware. In the well-known, often anthologized Section II ("Morning Song"), he achieves a richness and variety of verbal harmony in

67

a sensuous painting of nature that makes Senlin's obliviousness to the miracle of man on earth profoundly moving. The aureate diction of the earlier poems—this time with a greater muscularity, but still not great—is appropriate. In his thinking on the nature of God he arrives nowhere. Insignificant as his thoughts may be, yet

> These thoughts are truer of god, perhaps,
> Than thoughts of god are true.

"The Pilgrimage of Festus," like "Senlin," is a clearer statement of the poet's purpose than is the earlier work. The faults of the poem are, however, the same faults—prolixity and the over-zealous attempt to make poetry do what is better done by music.

A poet must love words, of course, and he must continue a relentless search for the right word to evoke the proper correspondence in the mind of the reader, but he must not forget the purpose of words—communication. In so far as he does forget, he fails. The moment he surrenders himself to the sheer luxury of indulgence in words for their own sake and for their emotive effect in combination divorced from meaning he is lost. He has become their slave instead of their master. His discipline is destroyed and with it significant form. This, I am afraid, is what happened to Mr. Aiken in these earlier long works. It is only by a slow process that he has to any extent extricated himself.

Although the metrical pattern of "John Deth" (1922-1924) is more regular than those of the poems in *The Divine Pilgrim*, he has chosen a form—the four-stress couplet—that is dangerous for its facility. Byron realized this in his Oriental Tales and finally abandoned it. The theme of the poem may possibly be expressed in the questions What is the meaning of life? What is beauty? For the thinker, death is a welcome release from the everlasting grief of life. As Millicent says:

> My life is yours; your will is law.
> And yet, eternal wing and claw,—

Franchise for everlasting grief,—
These seek I not! Better the brief
And dumb existence of the leaf.
Who knows nought—let him live forever!
Who knows and mourns—pity! and sever
From the blind sap that bears him, lord;
Deep death alone is his reward . . .

—p. 67.

In this poem, too, words are used for their musical values rather than for their utilitarian potentialities. And by utilitarian, I mean the effective communication of a clearly thought out idea.

In *Preludes for Memnon* (1931) Mr. Aiken achieves a greater muscularity in his rhythms than he has previously done in any of his long poems, and attempts to answer the questions "Who am I?" "What is reality?" "What is the meaning of life?"— questions which have beaten insistently on his brain. He is tormented by the meaninglessness of life and confused in his attempts to see his position in this meaningless universe.

Poor fool, sad anthromorph, give up this notion
Centrifugal; perpend awhile, instead,
The world centripetal, and see yourself
As the last corner in this world of shapes.
You dream the world? Alas, the world dreamed you.
And you but give it back, distorted much
By the poor brain-digestion, which you call
Intelligence, or vision, or the truth.

—p. 22.

If you have courage to pursue knowledge to its limits "it is to self you come—And that is God." There is nothing in the beginning, nothing at the end, "and in between these useless nothings, brightness, music, God, one's self." And if this self be probed objectively we realize that

69

There is no good,
No sweet, no noble, no divine, no right,
But it is bred of rich economy
Amongst the hothead factions of the soul

—p. 59.

Naturally, in the sixty-two preludes, the poet has looked at the questions from every point of view, although, perforce, he must arrive at the same conclusion. He continues his examination in *Time In The Rock* (1936), which he subtitles *Preludes to Definition*. It is difficult neatly to crystallize the universal questions to which he seeks an answer, although it has been suggested that they are "What shall I think?", "What shall I do?", "What is my relation to the entire world?" These are accurate enough, and the answers, in general, are that the only reality lies within a man's self and not in his outward relations; that man, like everyone and everything else, is constantly changing and must necessarily always be alone; and that before he can express his ideas, he must first solve the problem of self, a solution to which he invariably arrives too late. Unfortunately, the statement of the themes and their development is not clear.

It is natural for a sensitive mind to concern itself with the mysteriousness of life, but it must not neglect more important matters, the problem of daily living. To dwell too insistently on these questions that are largely unanswerable is as much an escape from reality as it is a struggle for reality. It seems to me that Mr. Aiken does not move forward, but in treadmill fashion. Granted the truth of what he says about God, about the meaninglessness of the universe, about man's pettinesses, the struggle with his blood—and he has attempted to follow the findings of the advanced thinkers of the past and present: Christ, Buddha, Confucius, Einstein, Freud, and others—he fails, it seems to me, to recognize what it is necessary to do. It is no little achievement to give meaning to meaninglessness by attempting to walk with dignity in the presence of the vast physical forces that constantly assail man both from without and within. He has needed Raphael's advice to Adam (*Paradise Lost*) that he should not solicit his thoughts too much with hidden matters, and he should remember "to know/That which before us lies in daily life,/Is the prime Wisdom."

It is apparent, both in *Preludes for Memnon* and *Time In The Rock*, that Mr. Aiken was striving for a firmer texture than he has achieved in his earlier work, a flatter music, one with more energy. He often achieves a staccato effect, but I think it would be erroneous to mistake it for vitality. Too often, particularly in *Time In The Rock*, he has given us rhetoric instead of poetry, and often very bad rhetoric at that. Sections XXXI to XXXV are particularly so, and occasionally we have such passages of alliteration as the following:

> *Then the red edge of sunlight spoke alone*
> *graving the stars until their granite grieved*
> *and groves of gardens grew along those grooves.*

Too often we encounter passages when his critical faculty that should have been most alert during the process of creation has been lulled into somnolence.

Thus far I have spoken only of Mr. Aiken's long poems written before World War II. Before considering his late work I think it necessary to retrace our steps and face an important question. If these long poems are largely failures, is there any work of his prior to 1940 that is not? I think there is. When Mr. Aiken is willing to subject himself to the discipline imposed by the desire for strict economy, he frequently achieves work of high merit. To me he has said in "Tetélestai" and "The Road" everything that he has said in his three early "symphonies" and said it with significant form. After years of close reading of these poems I still find them moving. So, too, do I find some of his love poems, but only a very few of his sonnets. "Music I heard with you," some of the sections from "Priapus and the Pool," one or two sonnets from *And In The Human Heart* (1940) will do more for his chances for immortality than will his more ambitious work. It seems to me, for example, that "Music I heard with you" is impeccable in its tone. By means of a simple but sensitively experienced diction, in a traditional strongly iambic four-line stanza, he has created a lyric of great beauty. It has sentiment, but line seven keeps it from sentimentality.

> *Music I heard with you was more than music,*
> *And bread I broke with you was more than bread;*
> *Now that I am without you, all is desolate;*
> *All that was once so beautiful is dead.*
>
> *Your hands once touched this table and this silver,*
> *And I have seen your fingers hold this glass.*
> *These things do not remember you, beloved,—*
> *And yet your touch upon them will not pass.*
>
> *For it was in my heart you moved among them,*
> *And blessed them with your hands, and with your eyes;*
> *And in my heart they will remember always,—*
> *They knew you once, O beautiful and wise.*

The remaining sections of "Discordants," from which the foregoing is taken, although superficially similar in music, fail because of faults of diction. It is obvious to any reader, I think, that the music of the foregoing is suitable only for a short lyric and not for a long poem.

No reader should underestimate Mr. Aiken's solid craftsmanship. A careful examination of the manuscript versions of a poem throw light on his methods. The changes in "Eclogue 3: All Death, All Love," for example, reveal his concern for accuracy of epithet as well as for his rhythms, especially his attempts to avoid the too facile iambs or anapests. Line eight of the original version—"the famous dead are brought, none comes to preach and bury" is changed to bring strong stresses together—"the famous dead come." In line five he had placed four strong stresses together "black gate lies open," but he later deleted "black." Most of Mr. Aiken's changes, however, are essentially verbal and indicate a striving for a sharper impact. "Ruby," for example, becomes "blood" in "spills amber and blood"; "tugging at earth, the splendid mother" is changed to "tugging at dark earth, like trees," then the "dark" is deleted. Frequently, the change is toward less aureate diction. "Skilled passion" passes to "bones and ruin" by the way of "hushed relics," and "embrace the dead" becomes "accept the dead." There is little tendency, however, as there was with Mr. Williams, of sharply reducing the original.

Since 1940, Mr. Aiken has published only two new volumes of poetry—*The Kid* (1947) and *Skylight One* (1949). In some ways they are a reversion to his earlier musical style. *The Kid* has little significance; *Skylight One* a little more. Both seem strangely out of the current of the best contemporary poetry— even that of the conservatives, although some of the poems in the latter volume have a nostalgic music. Mr. Aiken has quite obviously said all that is within him to say by means of verse.

A question naturally arises. Why has Mr. Aiken not accomplished more? He has the requisite intellectual and poetic equipment to have done better; and he had the leisure. I think the answer lies in the fact that having too much leisure he has devoted himself too exclusively to poetry. He has obtained much of his subject matter vicariously rather than from life. Only occasionally does the reader feel that closeness with the earth that vitalizes all great poetry. Knowing little about his private life, I nevertheless feel that his contacts have been too circumscribed. He has too willingly accepted the idea of the meaninglessness of life, and his acceptance enervated him. He has too easily given way to despair, and as too easily escaped from it:

> *I have known*
> *Such sunsets of despair as god himself*
> *Might weep for of a Sunday; and then slept*
> *As dreamlessly as Jesus in his tomb.*
> *—Preludes for Memnon*, p. 94.

73

He has been too prone to believe that "habitual strength is no stronger than habitual weakness" and that "the habitual hero is no hero." Perhaps he has been too easily content. Mr. Aiken will be known to most readers through anthologies. The few who will seek to extend their knowledge of his poetry will find disappointment. He will be remembered as a writer of a few unforgettable lyrics and shorter poems, not as a philosophical poet.

Mark Van Doren
1894—

Mr. MARK VAN DOREN'S first published
volume of poems, *Spring Thunder and Other Poems* (1924), re-
vealed a poet of keen perception and delicate sensitivity, with a
sound respect for the craftsmanship of verse. The promise of this
first volume was supported by the second, *7 P.M. and Other
Poems* (1926). The subject matter was extended, the craftsmanship became more secure, and a depth of feeling, not apparent
in the first volume, appeared. Subsequent volumes have been
disappointing. The subject matter has been extended, his craftsmanship within the scope of traditional forms has improved, but
the essential ingredient of poetry—the passionate conviction
that what the poet has to say is significant—is lacking. One of
the reasons for this is obvious—he has written too much. Rarely
is a poem charged with the emotion that it unconsciously acquires
when the poet has struggled for significant form. I do not wish
to imply that a poem should be, as one modern poet said, un-
understandable. I have no sympathy with the cult of the obscure
or of the tortured phrase, but I do believe the poet must achieve
a tautness of inner tension that communicates itself to the reader.
Too often Mr. Van Doren's poetry seems to be written for the
easy reader, the person who thinks that by reading a narrative
in verse he is achieving a greater stature than by reading a narrative in prose.

Mr. Van Doren has been content to work within the great
tradition of poetry rather than to seek to alter it, as so many of
the poets in the present volume have done. This is not to say,
however, that he has made no innovations or that he differs in
no way from other poets writing in traditional forms. His
knowledge of our earlier poetry, particularly that of the seven-

75

teenth century, has given him a profounder understanding of the subtleties of that tradition than are possessed by most poets. Specifically, he is not fooled into thinking that the iambic line was the model used by most of the poets. The variation of his rhythms and stresses is greater than the casual reader would realize, and closely corresponds with the rhythms of speech. In his first volume, it was the speech rhythms as crystallized in Mr. Frost's poetry. The details of "Travelling Storm," the final two lines of "Spring Thunder"—"There! Did you hear the edge/ Of winter crumble?" and all of "Former Barn Lot" are typically Frostian, especially this last:

> *Once there was a fence here,*
> *And the grass came and tried,*
> *Leaning from the pasture,*
> *To get inside.*
>
> *But colt feet trampled it,*
> *Turning it brown;*
> *Until the farmer moved*
> *And the fence fell down.*
>
> *Then any bird saw,*
> *Under the wire,*
> *Grass nibbling inward*
> *Like green fire.*

Not only is the attribution to the bird of the sight of what was taking place right, but the simile is fresh and vivid. "Afterward" and "Marriage" also reveal a sympathetic and understanding nature which has received a great hurt.

In Section III of *7 P.M. and Other Poems*, the lyrics on love have a more passionate tone than the poems in the first volume. "By-Laws," for example, is true of every sensitive lover. The tone of "First Night Alone," "Burial," and "The Sage in the Sierra" accords with the subject of each. In the last, particularly, the freer form carries conviction and marks a deepening of the poet's powers.

When we approach the poems in *Now the Sky and Other Poems*, it seems to me that Mr. Van Doren has relaxed his effort and begins to be satisfied with less than a perfect fusion of subject into significant form. "We Come Too Late" illustrates what I mean. Instead of mixing three types of verse which do not support the subject matter, he should have hammered out for himself a verse better fitted to make an impact than the ones he has chosen; or he should have sought more diligently among the traditional forms. The poem begins well in a four-stress unrhymed verse, but soon changes to others. Elsewhere in this same volume he uses two or more prosodic schemes in the poem, but I think unsuccessfully. He seems to be striving for a less derivative form of expression than was evident in the first two volumes, but he has not succeeded. The spontaneity has vanished. The stanza form used in "Defeated Farmer" does not support the subject. "Death," "The Crowd," "Pastoral," and, particularly, "Man" are, however, well-integrated wholes. But my general reaction to the volume is that in spite of his metrical competence, Mr. Van Doren has failed in the effort necessary to raise a poem from a competent one to a genuinely good one. A pedestrianism is too often evident. The reader, soon aware of the objectivity of the poet, arising from the fact that he is an observer not a participator, reads on hoping for a poem which will spring to life taking him with it; but he reads on in vain.

Delaying for a moment consideration of his long narrative poem, "Jonathan Gentry" and of "A Winter Diary," let us consider the sonnets and later lyrics.

The sonnets, expressing the common experience of everyone in love, reflect a cool, restrained ardour. The poet talks about his great passion, but he fails to express it. Nowhere does the reader sense the exercise of restraint on the part of the poet. I do not mean, of course, that they have the unbridled quality of Miss Wylie's love sonnets, but rather that he has no real passion to restrain. It is obvious from the subject matter that his is not so demonstrative a nature as that of the girl for whom the sonnets are written and that she has been the one who has taken the initiative. The following—one of the better sonnets—reveals with each reading that any passion in the poet is cerebral. It is cold and lacking in muscularity:

> *All of the steps that our slow love has taken*
> *Were your own steps at last, who led the way.*
> *I was too fixed—or like an oak was shaken*
> *That was marked to fall yet never may.*
> *Never unless you taught me had I known it:*
> *Love must be advancing or it dies.*
> *You found each resting-place, but had outgrown it*
> *Before I too was ready to arise.*
> *Love is a journey to no end, except*
> *One traveller, halting, cannot journey more.*
> *When I awoke you had as wisely stepped*
> *As the sole fox across a forest floor;*
> *So I would always follow you; and will*
> *To the last hedge upon the highest hill.*

Granted that the foregoing is competent verse—except possibly for the final four lines which give no sense of inevitability—the reader never has the impression that the sonnet is not a large enough form for the expression of his thought. It is almost too ample for his needs.

Frequently Mr. Van Doren is successful in his definitions. Those of "Wit" or "Praise," for example, are excellent. In "Joy Cannot Be Contained," however, unless I fail entirely to grasp what he is doing, the poem seems more suited to pain than to joy. But the characteristic that seems to be increasingly lacking in the lyrics of this period is sharpness of detail. The effect of "On Such A Day As This One" depends on the movement of the verse rather than on anything explicitly stated. Too much is left to the freedom of the reader's imagination. Among the best of the lyrics are such as "Time and Water," "The Other House," "Recognition Scene," and "The Monument" which cover a multiplicity of subjects. The poet's subject matter is indeed catholic and is perhaps best expressed in his imitation of

Herrick's opening to the *Hesperides*, which he, however, places at the close, and has fittingly titled "The End."

Although the same charges could be made against the poems in *The Last Look and Other Poems* as have been made in the foregoing, the details are not quite the same. We do have a rather weak echo of Mr. Ransom's "Here Lies a Lady" in "How Such a Lady," but we also have lyrics in which Mr. Van Doren is uniquely himself. "Axle Song" supports the idea, evident elsewhere, that he is not slavishly tied to the iamb in the way that second-rate versifiers seem too often to be. He is interested in the stresses and does not believe that every line with the same number of syllables necessarily contains the same number of stresses. To emphasize this would be supererogation were not too many literary historians and critics still inclined to fit stanzas into the Procrustean bed of classical feet, allowing always, of course, they say, for the substitutions permitted for the iamb. The Midas-ears are still numerous among us. Such poems as "Inarticulate," "The Last Look," "The Breathing Spell," and "Night's End" better illustrate his prosody than does "Axle Song." Although even in most of these the stanza form does not give the sense of inevitability, it more nearly does in "Night's End," of which the following is the first stanza:

Young man of many sorrows, do you know

How nar-row the sweet night is, and how soon

This hemi-sphere a-bove you will be split,

Let-ting light in, the mon-ster; let-ting clear waves

Shat-ter the scen-ted cloud? Do you, the feast-er,

Know the great air as taste-less on the tongue?

79

In his "analyses" to the poems in his *Introduction to Poetry*, it is clear that he rejects the system which scans the first line as iambic pentameter. The same is true of the "Changeling" with four stresses in the opening line rather than three as the Saintsburys would have it. Unless the reader is aware of Mr. Van Doren's sensitive handling of stresses he will miss much of the charm and richness of many of the lyrics.

Although an occasional lyric would tend to disprove the charge—witness "Inarticulate," "Porch God," "Driveway God," and perhaps others in which the images are frequently excellent—the impression I have from these later lyrics is that the poet has been too content with easy epithets rather than displaying the willingness to expend the effort to crystallize them vividly or to make them sharply evocative. He would seem to have become aware of this himself, because in *The Seven Sleepers* he strives for a tightening of structure and a greater sharpness in the images. This is evident in "The Single Sleeper," "Total War," "Truth Waits." He seems, too, to have striven for and achieved a crisper rhythm, one that is not so monotonously soothing. He begins to react to the prosodic experiments of some of the *avant garde*, although his reaction is a conservative one. Traces of it occur in "The Double Life," the ironic "Autonomous," "The Diarist," "Old Style," "The Pond Ages," "This Boy and Girl," and others. On the whole, however, the effect is slight. *New Poems* marks no advance over the former volumes. Unless the reader regards as important anything the poet may say, he will dip into the volume only to lay it aside.

A glance at one of Mr. Van Doren's manuscripts reveals, however, that his poems were the result of a careful reworking. The holographs of "The Picture," or "Ambush," or of "Problem," for example, are almost undecipherable because of the author's changes. It is interesting, however, but characteristic, I think, that the changes are not for rhythmical purposes, but solely for the sake of sharper impact. And it is, of course, the monotony of much of Mr. Van Doren's music that tires the reader.

Mr. Van Doren has written three long poems: "Jonathan Gentry," "Winter Diary," and "The Mayfield Deer," the first and third narratives, the second descriptive. I found "Winter Diary" dull and lacked the incentive to finish it. Its interest would be purely regional. "Jonathan Gentry," like Benèt's "John Brown's Body" and "Western Star," is in several metres. For the most part, the transition from one to the other is easily encompassed, but at times the abrupt intrusion of rhymed stanzas is disturbing. I found such to be the case at pages 108, 110, 114, but effective at page 137 of the poem as printed in *Collected Poems*. Many of the songs, however, are effective. The poem, in three parts, describes the founding of the family in 1800, the participation of Jonathan Gentry III in the Civil War, and the last of the line because of the barrenness of the wife of Jonathan Gentry V. Although the story held my interest, I felt that the poet's treatment lacked real dramatic power. The movement of the verse, again competent, fails to compensate for the lack of psychological insight that a good novelist would give it. It lacked the dimensional quality that it needs. Some subjects lend themselves better to a long poem than they do to a novel, others not. I cannot imagine, for example, *Paradise Lost* or *Samson Agonistes* as novels, because the poetry more than atones for any details or psychological subtleties that may be lacking. The Jonathan Gentry saga is, however, ill suited to its form. As is the case with so many long narrative poems, I feel the form was chosen to conceal the technical inability of the author to treat his subject matter as it should be treated. In "The Mayfield Deer," Mr. Van Doren has wisely confined himself to one metre. Otherwise, what I have said about "Jonathan Gentry" applies to this later narrative. His model, conscious or unconscious, was Edwin Arlington Robinson, an unfortunate model, because *The Mayfield Deer* has the same prolixity, the same questionable psychology, the same tediousness as any one of Robinson's long narrative poems. Quite possibly the subject matter is better fitted to a long poem than was the material of the Gentry saga. Mr. Van Doren's treatment of it, however, is a failure. Rarely have I read anything that interested me less. Again, as in most of his poetry, the verse is competent, but it rarely rises above the level of mere competence.

Many readers may feel that I have been too severe on Mr. Van Doren. Perhaps I have. It is possible, however, that the newer rhythms of the *avant garde* poets have made it impossible for me to enjoy today what I may have enjoyed twenty-five years ago, or even fifteen. Their best work, however, has a tautness that I fail to find in his. To the reader who may perhaps wonder what the effect of the rhythms of the *avant garde* poets has had on my appreciation of the earlier poets, I can say that I can now better appreciate the freedom of the rhythms of the earlier centuries than ever before, except perhaps for much of the work of the nineteenth century, a period now ripe for a thorough re-valuation. The rhythms of the *avant garde* poets have also re-vealed the gross inadequacy of the nineteenth-century writers on prosody such as Saintsbury. Mr. Van Doren, however, will suffer the fate of many of the Georgians. He is too much the cool observer, too much the disinterested scholar to invest his subject matter with the passion necessary to make his work spring to life. It is not that a person cannot be urbane and still be a good poet. But behind this urbanity there must exist a passionate conviction for the truth of those things one chooses to write about. I do not sense this conviction in Mr. Van Doren. Mr. Ransom is equally urbane with a greater elegance and seeming aloofness, but be-hind that façade is a passionate conviction of the truth about what he writes. He has remained, therefore, the greater artist, even though he has published no poetry in over ten years. Mr. Van Doren should long ago have curbed his prolixity. Perhaps there is still time for him to do so. Unless he does so, he must be content to have as his readers lovers of verse rather than of poetry. The fault is not that he has used traditional forms, but that he has failed to inspirit them with new vitality. He has failed in the quality of empathy. He is aware of the minutiæ as well as of the grander aspects of nature; he is interested in all types of persons, and in all situations; he adds details of the

American scene that are interesting. His attitude toward all these things, however, is that of a describer of them in verse rather than that of a "maker," and no one knows better than he from his appreciation of other "makers" the qualities that such a term implies. He should turn his critical eye inward past the problem of mere structural form to that of significant form.

Robert Silliman Hillyer
1895—

I N an age of acute social consciousness, rapid change, and often of startling experiment in atonality and obscurity, the poetry of Mr. Robert Hillyer may seem to be an anomaly. Surveyed from the point of view of the sheer number of volumes of verse, near-poetry, and poetry that issue from the smaller presses as well as those of a more solid reputation, it is the poets of the *avant garde* that would seem to be the anomaly rather than he because from that point of view American poetry is almost stultifyingly traditional. Mr. Hillyer has been content to work in the English lyrical tradition rather than to extend that tradition by attempting to assimilate foreign rhythms to those of English and American speech. Because what he does is less dramatic and spectacular than those things accomplished by bolder experimenters, the solid merits of his achievement are sometimes understated.

Before attempting an evaluation of his work, let me first clear away certain useless lumber. He has in some measure, but not wholly, assisted us. *The Collected Verse* (1933) contains all the work from his earlier volumes that he wished to preserve. Subsequent volumes are *A Letter to Robert Frost* (1937), *Pattern of a Day* (1940), *Poems for Music* (1947), and *The Death of Captain Nemo* (1949). *Poems for Music* contains about forty-five of the best lyrics from *The Collected Verse* and *Pattern of a Day* in addition to others. The selection reveals a keener self-criticism than is possessed by most poets. Before turning our attention to these lyrics, however, let us glance briefly at the rest of the work.

Mr. Hillyer has attempted two long poems: *Alchemy* (1920)

and *The Death of Captain Nemo* (1949). Both unsuccessful, they reveal all too clearly the fact that he does not possess the qualities of sustained thought and passionate intensity requisite for a long poem. Only in one passage does he rise above the level of competency—an invective against the average American's attitude toward his country, and as political as anything he ever wrote (pp. 19, 20). Unfortunately, however, the other fifty-five pages of the poem provide weak sustenance to anyone save the dreamer.

The lack of solid and significant subject matter is less evident in his epistolary satires than elsewhere. The exigencies of the heroic couplet demand a tightness of texture and an incisiveness of perception that are lacking in all but his best lyrics. Each of the epistles contains good things, but suffers from a flabbiness of form. As he remarks in "A letter to Robert Frost," he takes an unconscionable time a-dying; or, as he noticed in "A Letter to Charles Townsend Copeland," he puts his audience to sleep. The central portions of these epistles are often excellent and reveal a genuine satiric gift and a delightful sense of humour and urbanity. The reader suspects, however, that Mr. Hillyer did not pursue this genre because he lacked subject matter over which he could sufficiently arouse himself. He is too gentle a person for sharp invective.

Anyone who has seen the holograph of "A Letter to Queen Nefertite" would hesitate to accuse Mr. Hillyer of a lack of concern for form. The manuscript reveals much tentative work, erasures, deletions, inserts, and so forth. It certainly did not write itself and the poet's third version remains almost undecipherable because of his changes. But a characteristic of the poet is sharpened by a glance at some of the reworked lines. "Against intrusions from an alien world" becomes much more evocative in its later form—"In secret fragrance from a wind-swept world." "The secret river secret in your smile" becomes "Curved in the furtive wisdom of your smile."

The youthful poems in such volumes as *The Five Books of Youth* (1920) and others, although better than most written by young poets in their early twenties, are better ignored. Mr.

85

Hillyer has, however, been a prolific writer of sonnets, both separate and in sequence. His efforts in this medium only serve to remind us how difficult it is to write a good sonnet and how few poets achieve a successful one. Although some of his are often good in part, I know of none that ranks with the greater English sonnets. Frequently the octave is good and the sestet inferior (*The Collected Verse*, 93, 98); or a part of a quatrain or sestet is felicitously phrased (*Ibid.*, 102, ll. 3-4, 106); or the figures are apt. On the other hand, some sonnets are downright bad (*Ibid.*, 107); or an image is awkward (*Ibid.*, 103, ll. 5-6), the expression trite, the music flat, or the rhymes disappointing. What is lacking in the sonnets in *The Collected Verse* is even more apparent in the sequence, "In Time of Mistrust" (*Pattern of a Day*, 68-81).

It is apparent from the foregoing that Mr. Hillyer's accomplishment lies within a narrow compass. I think his poetic reputation will depend upon about thirty lyrics out of the seventy in *Poems for Music*. Let us, therefore, concentrate our attention on these. After all, thirty good lyrics is no mean achievement. It is apparent from "Unregimented" that the poet is unwilling to proselytize for any specific political cause; he prefers to be a "triumphant Quietist." What, then, comprises the subject matter of his poetry? A few poems deal directly or indirectly with the subject of poetry, a few with love, with birds mythical or otherwise, with sheer fantasy. He gives a few excellent vignettes; but the majority deal with the subject of nature in all her moods, times of day, and differences of season. Without being in any way directly reminiscent of Herrick, he is the poet with whom Mr. Hillyer has the greatest affinity. But he wears his lyricism with a difference. The two modern poets of whose influence I am conscious are Robert Frost and John Crowe Ransom, that of Mr. Frost being much the greater. It permeates "The Watchdog" in epithet, diction and music, and yet is not a slavish imitation. It is also present in "The Deserted Farmhouse" and "The Assassination." It would probably be more accurate to say that Mr. Frost has shown a younger New Englander one road to take, and it was a road that the elder poet had not followed to the end. "The Untended Field," for example, is a poem that could only be understood by a person deeply familiar with New England, and particularly northern New England. The strong regular beat of the lines, the hard, masculine rhymes with their long vowels, the sense of the futility of resisting the "green stampedes" flung by the "wind and sun and rain" combine to create the sense of the inevitableness of the encroachment of the forest on the abandoned field. Mr. Ransom's influence is purely a prosodic one. It is very distinct in "Elegy: On a Dead Mermaid Washed Ashore at Plymouth Rock" and less so in "The Seagoing Farmer." But I do not mention this to minimize these poems, both of which reveal great mastery of the lyrical idiom by Mr. Hillyer. The romantic mood of fantasy is well caught in the subtle manipulation of sounds in the closing lines of "Elegy: On a Dead Mermaid Washed Ashore at Plymouth Rock":

> *Now ocean reclaims you again, lest a marvel so tragic*
> *Remain to be mocked by our earthly and virtuous eyes,*
> *And reason redeems already what seems*
> *Only a fable like all our strange and beautiful dreams.*

The music of "The Seagoing Farmer" is less mellifluous than that of "Elegy" and less consciously derivative and tells with humour the romantic longings of the farmer, so similar to those of the younger brother in *Beyond the Horizon.*

Most of the lyrics in *Poems for Music* would seem to be Mr. Hillyer's attempt to counteract the great defect of our age as he has expressed it in "XXth Century":

> *There is no time,*
> *No time,*
> *There is no time,*
> *Not even for a kiss,*
> *Not even for this,*
> *Not even for this rhyme.*

There may be no time for others to do these things, but he

would make time for himself. He would not only do this but he would convince the sceptics that the rewards of those who insist on finding the time *to be* are greater than those who feel there is only time *to do*. This is in one sense explicitly the meaning of "Andante Simplice," but it is also inherent in most of the others. The mood is one of peace, serenity, and gentleness.

I think it would be true to say of Mr. Hillyer that no modern poet depends so little on what is actually said (that is, as it could be paraphrased) and so much on the way of saying it. Since the variations in mood are less from subject matter than from expression, let us examine some of the devices by which he achieves his effects.

It is obvious that Mr. Hillyer has made a careful study of rhythms. His deft mastery of them is everywhere apparent. His stanza forms vary from those of two to five stresses, from four verses to many, the most frequent being the ballad stanza. At times, however, the stanza is composed of lines of irregular length with an irregular inweaving of rhymes. Internal as well as end rhymes are important in his lyrical scheme. Whereas it is readily apparent that a musical notation is necessary to capture the subtle nuances of time in the best work of Pound, Williams, Ransom, and Auden, it is not so obvious that the traditional notation of iambs, anapests, trochees, and so forth, fails to give an adequate notation for those of Mr. Hillyer.

The most recurrent stylistic device in the lyrics is repetition. It may be in extremely small units, or it may be in more extended units. Assonance occurs frequently, for example, as in "flicker and quiver"; so, too, does alliteration. Often the repetition is of syllables, or of all the foregoing taken together, as in the last stanza of "Lost Twilight":

There was a time-less time that seems

One with the foot-fall of my dreams,

♪ | ♩ ♪ | ♪. ♪: | ♩ ♪ | ♩.
Yet I remember it as well

♪ | ♪. ♪. | ♩ ♪ | ♪ ♪ | ♩.
As echoes from a silent bell

| ♩ ♪ | ♪. | ♪ ♪. : ♪. ♪ | ♩.
Or the sea soun-ding in a shell

| ♪. | ♩ ♪ | ♩. ♪ | ♪. ♪ | ♩.
Words fail when we would say these things,

♪. | ♩ ♪ | ♩ ♪ | ♩ ♪ | ♩.
No phrase there is that speaks or sings,

♪ | ♪. ♪ | ♩ ♪ | ♩. : ♪ ♩. | ♩.
And what we know we can-not tell.

Even though it is clear that there are many regular iambs in the
foregoing, it is equally clear that a notation that includes the
temporal reveals subtleties otherwise obscure. The stanza could
be scanned as regularly four-stress throughout, but I think that
reading the first, fifth, sixth, and seventh lines with five stresses
brings out delicacies of modulation that otherwise remain un-
noted. Liquids and nasals abound, of course, in the foregoing.

Internal rhyme plays, too, as I have suggested, an important
role in his musical scheme, often the rhymes being on liquids.
Two examples from "The Deserted Farmhouse" are sufficient:

| ♩. | ♩. | ♩. ♪ ♪ | ♪ ♩ | ♩.
Stale, damp mould in the lifeless cold

| ♩ ♪ | ♩. ♩ ♪ | ♩. | ♩. | ♩.
Darkness spills from the wild, bleak hills.

The most characteristic use of repetition, however, is that on
words. Let us select five examples which will illustrate far more
effectively than could a prose commentary. In the final line of
each stanza of "Reunion," the two "farewells" are repeated; but

their different positions in the line indicate the disillusionment that is a natural part of a class reunion.

(1) The clock ticked on. *Farewell, farewell.*
(2) *Farewell.* The clock ticked on. *Farewell.*
(3) *Farewell, farewell.* The clock ticked on.

Let us admit that this is an obvious device in a poem that is not one of the poet's best, but it nevertheless reveals that it is a conscious device.

It is more subtly used in "A Soft November Night":

How can November thus
Be summer? summer fabulous?
While soft as a feather, soft as snow
Or snowy moonlight on moonlit eaves
One cricket weaves the winds together.

The repetition of "shadow" in "Reflections in Still Water" contributes greatly to the somnolent quality of the poem:

I watched the pond without lifting my eyes;
Shadows of leaves on shadow skies;
Scarves of colour twining through haze
And a bright bird flying with wings ablaze;
A bird flying over, the day in flight,
And I watched him pass without lifting my eyes.
It was enough, the shadow of delight,
The shadow of a bird over shadow skies.

The first white star unbound her hair;
The water trembled, and she was there
Setting her foot on the darkening mirror
While round her the trees of night leaned nearer;
They gathering dark, she gathering light,
And I watched the pond without lifting my eyes;
It was enough, the shadow of night,
The shadow of a star in the shadow skies.

The repetition is of a different quality in "Andante Simplice," and is essentially in the nature of consonance. Speaking of the rays of morning striking the flower-girl, the poet says that they

> *. . . twinkle on anklets*
> *That jangle together*
> *With tinkle of bells*
> *And melodious jingle*
> *As gay as a robin and clear as a thrush.*

The wind, too, is awake with her

> *With songs of the sunrise that mingle*
> *With singing of birds in the willow.*

Mr. Hillyer is well aware that his lute is old and that its silver strings are almost mute in the blare of horn and clarion. But he believes his music will outlast the more strident music of the brasses; and I am prone to agree with him. The music of "Light Snowfall," "Wild Ducks Drifting," "It is Easy to Forget a Song," "Night Piece," "A Song for the Beloved" is music for the lute. So, too, is "Folk Song: Elegy." Here he achieves a striking effect by altering the rhythm from the iambic of the second line—"The lily and the rose"—with its three stresses to one of four stresses in a line of five syllables—"No lily, no rose." Lute music need not be unvaried or dull.

At times certain unpleasant questions force themselves into the reader's mind. Is too much of Mr. Hillyer's poetry, for example, escapist poetry? Does too much of it verge on decadence? This is not true of the charming "Madrigal," "An Invitation," or "Original Sin," nor of "The Tryst," "The Dark Ocean," or of most of the poems about nature already mentioned. The question comes to the fore, however, in "At Anchor," "The Demigod," and "Summer's Fool." In "At Anchor," for example, he speaks of himself as

. . . I am one who rests content
When masts are bare and sails furled,
Knowing the way the wind went
After it blew me from the world.

The question of decadence is particularly apropos to "The Demigod":

I wearied of disaster,
I swore to murder Fate,
And make myself the master
Of my terrene estate.

I slew my foe and gaily
Supplanted him I slew,
And do more damage daily
Than Fate could ever do.

—and to "Summer's Fool."

Dare a poet who has any real concern for poetry as a vital ingredient in our culture take such an attitude? Should not a poet lead the reader toward rather than away from a greater reality? If poetry has lost some of its high standing, are not the poets themselves to blame? Never did poetry hold so exalted a position as it did with the Greeks when the poets recognized their responsibility to make it a repository for the highest ideals of the Greek character. Until modern poets reaffirm and accept such a responsibility they can expect their audience to be small. This does not mean that poetry must assume either a pious or a didactic tone; but it does mean that the poets must themselves find the way to the abundant life as well as have under their complete control the instrument for communicating with passion what they find. Mr. Hillyer has control of the instrument, but there are too few things except the quietude of nature about which he has any deep convictions.

Allen Tate
1899—

THE milieu of Mr. Allen Tate's poetry is the
South; the dominant theme, the spiritual decay of America resulting from the increasing materialism of its culture. The theme
leads the poet into many by-roads—the meaning of life, the
meaning of death, the route to a spiritual regeneration, the problem of the person who refuses to submit to the stultifying forces
of this materialism, and many others. The theme is stated
directly, as well as obliquely; clearly as well as obscurely; pas-
sionately as well as dryly. The common reader's choice, however,
is restricted. Of the poems that have more than a craftsman-like
quality, the majority are too obscure for any reader except the
specialist who is willing to spend more time than the rewards
merit. Good poetry is difficult because it is unique. Once, however, the novelty of the poet's idiom has been grasped and the
reader's ear adjusted to the new music, the difficulties should
disappear, and in their place a broadened æsthetic experience
should succeed. That is not true with the most difficult of Mr.
Tate's poems. Instead of a broadened æsthetic experience, the
reader encounters aridity. This is not to say that such poems
offer nothing. They may provide an exciting image, an esoteric
allusion that flatters the reader's erudition, or an interesting
rhythm. What they do not offer is the well-integrated æsthetic
experience that one has a right to expect from a work of art. As
Miss Marianne Moore has remarked, "Enigmas are not poetry."
The foregoing requires justification and some modification, but
first mitigation of the harshness. Poems like "Mediterranean,"
"To the Lacedemonians," "Ode to the Confederate Dead,"

93

"Emblems," "Retrodution to American History," "Fragment of a Meditation," "Winter Marsh," and a few others offer few difficulties and can afford much pleasure. Even these, however, lack the warmth and graciousness found in the best work of Mr. Ransom and Mr. Warren, with whom Mr. Tate is invariably linked. One cause may lie in the poet's creative habits.

Mr. Tate is a conscientious craftsman and has sought in his revisions to strengthen his poetic impact. At times the changes are minor, a "which" to a "that," an alteration of a single line, or an altered punctuation. Occasionally, however, the changes are extensive as in "A Pauper," "Obituary," and notably "Ode to the Confederate Dead." In this latter poem, the changes have enhanced the clarity and poetic impact.

Mr. Tate is aware of the necessity for inner tension in a poem, and he strives to achieve this. I do not think, however, that he often succeeds. I think I can explain what I mean by reference to such poems as "The Wolves," "The Subway," "The Eagle," "Last Days of Alice," and others. At first reading these are very difficult. The symbols are not only unfamiliar but the diction is concentrated. The general idea is relatively clear, but the details are difficult to comprehend. The reader has the vague feeling that could he unravel the details and then reconstruct the poem he would achieve an æsthetic experience that merited the effort. This feeling grows as he succeeds in solving the problems. He experiences the same type of pleasure as in solving a double acrostic. Once he has satisfied himself, however, and returns later to the poem with full understanding of the details, he discovers to his surprise that the ideas stand forth clearly but the tension which he at first suspected has disappeared and he is left with a sense of being cheated. Instead of a poem he is left with a *tour de force* and a prose statement. What are the details of this prose statement?

Mr. Tate decries the material culture of America and longs for the greater spirituality which he thinks can only be achieved by an escape from our highly industrialized cities to the soil. The

present generation, said the old soldier in "To the Lacedemonians," were sired by motion on a street corner. They
have never really been born. In his own day "the mere
breed" did not absorb the generation. Modern man has lost
the capacity to feel the "bright course of blood along the vein,"
they

> *. . . expect too much, do too little,*
> *Put the contraption before the accomplishment*
> *Lack skill of the interior mind*
> *To fashion dignity with shapes of air.*

He supplies details to this bitterly realistic attitude in "Jubilo,"
"Winter Marsh," "Retroduction to American History," and
"Causerie." The rhythms are dry, rapid, conversational. Because
the reader has not first to scale the wall of unintelligibility, he
will enjoy these poems for what they appear to be and not bring
as austere a critical analysis to them as he will to those where
the challenge has been greater.

In "The Wolves," "The Subway," and "The Eagle," the
statement is more bitter. He is not deluded into thinking the
golden-haired lad lying on the bed is different from the other
men about him. They are all snarling wolves. When such is the
case there can be no hope and man can have no dignity. In fact,
he believes that modern man is little more than an empty abstraction. The poet finds himself alone, or nearly so, because the
strong heart can never be subdued by the diseased mind or a
corrupt civilization.

To regain the significance of life, man must return to nature,
the mind to fundamentals, because life is more than mere sensa-
tion; it is thoughts about those sensations, for a proper evaluation
of which his roots must be in the earth. He must not dwell in
the past, but build upon the past for today and the future. Above
all, he must be true to himself ("The Trout Map," "The Meaning of Life," "The Meaning of Death").

In his increasing egocentricity man has lost all sense of God, to regain which it would be desirable to have a sense of sin ("Last Days of Alice"). This idea receives added poignancy in "The Twelve" which describes the world-wandering of the twelve apostles although they have lost all memory of Christ, are spiritually barren with nothing to say. Even when the poet himself struggles to recover this lost sense he realizes he has pursued a will-o'-the-wisp ("Ignis Fatuus").

Mr. Tate is not always directly concerned with such ideas. "Mother and Son," "Inside and Outside," and "Death of Little Boys" deal with death; "Shadow and Shade" is a love poem, "Homily," as I read it, is on insomnia or bad dreams, and "A Pauper" describes the sense of pathos which the pauper inspires but of which he is unaware.

Quite obviously the subject matter is that of a thoughtful and sensitive person. The problem for us, therefore, is to see how he integrates this subject matter with his genres, verse forms, diction, imagery and other details to achieve significant form. The weakest poems in *Poems: 1922-1947* are the sonnets, those "At Christmas" being inferior to "Sonnets of the Blood," themselves failures—and "Eclogue of the Liberal and the Poet," for which I can see little excuse. None of these possess sufficient inner tension to support the genre. In most other instances, however, Mr. Tate rises above mere competent craftsmanship. The blank verse of "Aeneas at Washington" may be somewhat reminiscent of Tennyson. Poems like "Ode to the Confederate Dead" with its irregular rhyme and "Mother and Son" (rhyming a-b-a-b-c-a-c) may strongly echo the rhythms of Mr. Ransom, but they are not slavishly imitative. Both are good poetry. "Causerie" has a more conversational tone. He employs too, a three-stress line in modified *terza rima* in "False Nightmare," and in a ten-line stanza in "Seasons of the Soul," a four-stress line in "Jubilo," "The Traveller," and "Pastoral," a five-stress one in stanzas of various arrangements of rhyme. In other words, variety is his prosodic characteristic.

His rhythms stem from many sources—the early Eliot, the mature Ransom, an occasional echo of Crane, of Donne and others in the English tradition, and once at least from Dante. The influence of Virgil is extensive. His diction is similarly derivative, paralleling the rhythms in their origins. Mr. Tate has been called a classic poet, but he is no more classic than Mr. Eliot. Both are arch-romantics. Let us admit, however, that the terms "classic" and "romantic" have little real meaning. In this instance, I am speaking of their attitudes toward life and in their too easy solution. The problem is simpler than a return to religion by the route of anglo-catholicism or to the soil. Mr. Tate's greatest originality reveals itself in his images.

"Death of Little Boys," a much anthologized poem, contains images of debatable validity. I find the poem satisfactory only if interpreted as the actual physical death of little boys and not as the symbolic death of little boys as they pass to manhood. The point of view is that, too, of the survivors. Even so, I find the simile in line three overwrought. That the event would "rage terrific as the sea" is improbable. I find overwrought, too, the image in lines seven and eight. I can visualize the "one peeled aster drenched with the wind" but I cannot understand the fear it excites. Stanza three conveys to me the last moments before death. Although the poet is consistent with his original intention he is forcing the image of the ship and sea. "Suspended breaths" as "white spars" is far-fetched. I feel that he fails completely with the much-praised image in stanza four. To speak of the boy as the "cliff of Norway" and as a "little town" that "reels like a sailor drunk in a rotten skiff" surpasses Wordsworth's characterization of a six-year-old as a "Mighty Prophet! Seer blest!" The only really satisfactory stanza is the final one.

In "Shadow and Shade," Mr. Tate attempts to carry the use of conceits and puns even farther than Donne who furnished the model for this poem. The poem begins well even though the first two lines are difficult—

The shadow streamed into the wall—
The wall, break-shadow in the blast;

They evoke in my mind the shadows of leaves and branches on a sunshiny wall. Then a cloud passes over the sky, putting the whole wall in shadow. At that point, the poet forgets Pandarus' advice to Troilus about the terms to be used in a love-letter—"ne scryvenyssh or craftily thou it write" nor "reherce it nought to ofte." He plays too much with his meaning of "shadow" and "shade." As the poem continues, the meaning shifts from the denotative to the connotative or symbolic and becomes associated with the lovers. In stanza five the sense shifts again, reaching its ultimate as a symbol of passion in the final stanza in which the man tells the woman at his side that unless they surrender themselves to this passion, they will "die alone." Although a clever *tour de force*, and a sustained example of metaphysical wit, the reader fails to sense the passion it would seem to describe. Perhaps "describe" rather than "communicate" is the cause of the lack of complete success.

A study of Mr. Tate's images would reveal much about the poet. The mind is "a windy apple . . . wormed," courage is "a white eagle," the heart of the average person is a "faggot," and his day instead of being bright is a "cinder." These are from "The Eagle," a poem clear enough in intention, but one in which the parts do not coalesce into an integrated whole. Not only are the images dark but his diction is often violent. The subway is a "plunger," ogives "burst," the noise is like an "exploding crucible." The energy which he attempts in poems like "The Subway," for example, is a forced rather than a native energy.

Of the poems requiring the closest scrutiny, "Last Days of Alice" is one of the most rewarding. Although it would always require close reading, it becomes clearer with each reading. The idea is developed steadily and skilfully with particular reference to Alice through the first seven stanzas, in which the looking-glass is a symbol of her complete absorption in herself. In stanza eight the poet shifts from Alice to a generalization on ourselves and in nine to the only solution by which we can regain our humanity. Lacking souls, devoid of spirituality, we are

> *a dumb shade-harried crowd*
> *Being all infinite, function depth and mass*
> *Without figure, a mathematical shroud*
> *Hurled at the air—blessed without sin!*

The association of man without spirituality to mathematics occurs elsewhere. In "The Subway," for example, he says "I am become geometries"—an abstraction rather than a real person.

Before returning to those poems on which Mr. Tate's reputation will assuredly rest, let us examine one other poem, "Mother and Son." Written in stanzas of varying lengths and with varying rhymes, it tells the story of the struggle between the mother at the bedside of her sick son and that son eager for death. The overwrought compression evident in several of the aforementioned poems is somewhat relaxed here, but only enough to give the poem its proper tone. And the tone is right. There is not the slightest suggestion of graciousness in the rhythms, nor ever a moment of the slightest lessening of the barrier between mother and son. Stanza two is a vivid presentation of the background. "Falcon" as an epithet for the mother in stanza three intensifies the heartless maternalism which she forces herself to show and which so relentlessly repels him. The image in which the workings of his fitful memory are likened to a "blind school of cuttlefish" which rise to the air and then sink far beneath the surface is excellent. The drama heightens in stanza five because of the intensity of the figures, particularly that not related to the drama itself, but to a phenomenon of nature—

> *The reaching sun, swift as the cottonmouth*
> *Strikes at the black crucifix on her breast*
> *Where the cold dusk comes suddenly to rest—*

The final stanza is effective because of the details the poet has chosen for the expression of the mood of hopeless futility.

In "Retroduction to American History" Mr. Tate achieves

a dry, rapid movement which, although deriving from Ransom, is uniquely his own. The images are not only accurate, but proportioned to the whole. In the first two paragraphs he creates the mood appropriate to the thoughts of disillusionment that crowd his wakefulness—the "stiff unhappy silence . . . struts like an officer." Then, aware that "antiquity breached mortality with myths," he re-examines the desiccation of these myths in modern society, and with sardonic humour decries the debasement of the humanistic values. We have become automata. How and when we shall again become human beings are questions he poses, but for which he has no answer.

> *Heredity*
> *Proposes love, love exacts language, and we lack*
> *Language. When shall we speak again? When shall*
> *The sparrow dusting the gutter sing? When shall*
> *This drift with silence meet the sun? When shall*
> *I wake?*

Too large a portion of society are the sparrows dusting the gutters.

It would be manifestly unfair to Mr. Tate to make no mention of "Ode to the Confederate Dead," one of his most successful poems, because in this poem he has effected a more harmonious fusion of thought, tone, feeling than in almost any other poem. Although he sees no cause for optimism, he is not bitter. There is sorrow instead, and also graciousness. The movement of the verse is deliberate but unremitting because of the irregular spacing of his rhymes and a sure sense for the placing of his caesurae. He employs epithets like "impunity," "scrutiny," "inexhaustible" with a fresh effect. The season is autumn, and the first two paragraphs recreate the scene with desolate hopelessness. At least the dead have fertilized the burying ground! He then compares by implication those who died for the Confederate cause with the living and questions the validity of their sacrifice. There is passionate statement in his question—

What shall we who count our days and bow
Our heads to a commemorial woe
In the ribboned coats of grim felicity,
What shall we say of the bones, unclean,
Whose verdurous anonymity will grow?

His answer holds little hope:

Night is the beginning and the end
And in between the ends of distraction
Waits mute speculation, the patient curse
That stones the eyes, or like the jaguar leaps
For his own image in a jungle pool, his victim.

The poem declines to a note of futility. Or is it acceptance and submission to the inevitable? "Why is it," he asks in "Winter Marsh" that

> *man hates*
> *His own salvation,*
> *Prefers the way to hell,*
> *And finds his last safety*
> *In the self-made curse that bore*
> *Him towards damnation:*
> *The drowned undrowned by the sea,*
> *The sea worth living for.*

It is readily apparent from the foregoing that I think Mr. Tate is a poet of a few poems, but that those few poems contain within themselves the power for survival. About half of the poems in *Poems: 1922-1947*, among them most of the sonnets, can be ignored with a consequent heightening of his reputation. Those in Section One, dealing particularly with the South, have a warmth that is only occasional elsewhere in the volume. In the intensity of his gaze at certain contemporary phenomena he has ignored the positive signs of an awakening spirituality in those groups where he sees none. His historical sights are too narrowly set. Many other poems in the volume fail in the communication of worthwhile ideas because of a too highly wrought idiom from which not only spontaneity but clarity have been excluded. They are too close to preciosity to appeal to more than the small coterie that have done so much harm to the cause of poetry. Instead of attempting to combat indifference—often a well-deserved indifference—they have provided additional reasons for an increased indifference. Such are as great enemies to poetry as those other practitioners of the art who have been content to express stalely their stale ideas, writing not so much to communicate their strongly experienced ideas as to satisfy their own petty egos. At his best Mr. Tate will assume his proper niche in the great tradition of poetry. What he says is worth saying and he is artist enough to know the value of form and craftsman enough to achieve it. Time will take care of his other work.

Laura Riding
1901—

B<small>Y</small> way of self-justification, Miss Laura Riding has made in the Introduction to her *Collected Poems* a curious statement of truth, partial-truth, perceptivity, pretentiousness, and utter nonsense. Instead of conciliating the reader it will annoy him, and, unless he has a greater than average persistence he will turn away. This is unfortunate, because much of Miss Riding's poetry is rewarding, some of it deeply so. It is not my intention to expound the truths and nonsense in Miss Riding's statement, but I must take issue with her on one important point. She has been accused of difficulty and obscurity, charges which she disclaims. "No readers but those who insist on going to poems for the wrong reasons should find my poems difficult," she says; "no reader who goes to poetry for the right reasons should find them anything but lucid; and with few other poets are readers so safe from being seduced into emotions or states of mind which are not poetic." It does not occur to her that the fault of obscurity may lie within her, that as an artist she has failed, that she is perhaps guilty of that of which she accuses others—that she has unconsciously been concerned "only with enjoying the display of [her] own faculties."

Miss Riding has a high concept of poetry. "A poem," she says, "is an uncovering of truth of so fundamental and general a kind that no other name besides poetry is adequate except truth. . . . Truth is the result when reality as a whole is uncovered by those faculties which apprehend in terms of entirety, rather than in terms merely of parts." I think she would look upon her poetry as educative, although not didactic, and would like to be thought a philosophical poet. Her concern is with universals, it is true, but I should be chary of calling her a philosophical poet. Let us admit, however, that this is essentially a problem in semantics.

The question "What is this poem about?" is, for Miss Riding, a vulgarism. Naturally, the complete poem can never be described, only read and experienced, but the common reader can approach her poetry with a greater possibility of understanding it if he knows the subjects that receive frequent treatment. At the risk of over-simplification I think we could say that the general categories are the nature and understanding of self, unity and the sense of oneness in the universe, death and immortality, the nature of reality and its relation to the imaginative world, time, spiritual barrenness, love, nature, as well as a miscellany of other or related ideas. Of the five sections under which she has arranged her poems, I have had greatest difficulty with those grouped as Poems of Final Occasion; least difficulty with Poems of Mythical Occasion and Poems Continual, the earliest and latest from point of view of chronology. The general reader would do well, I believe, to make his first acquaintance with Miss Riding's poetry by way of "The Troubles of a Book," "Rhythms of Love," "In Due Form," the third of "Three Sermons to the Dead," "The Last Covenant," "No More Than Is," "Friendship on Visit," "A Letter to Any Friend," and "When Love Becomes Words." Not only are these more likely to strike the note of common experience but the poet's statement is more direct, profoundly experienced, and less forced than elsewhere. These poems more nearly fall into the great tradition of English poetry than do others, but at no time is Miss Riding, any more than is Miss Moore, traditional. The two women disregard the tradition, however, in opposite ways: Miss Moore by an over-attention to minute detail, Miss Riding by neglecting the little details of common experience that would enable the reader to follow her; both, in their lack of interest in the subtle modifications in verse as a result of attempting to adjust the traditional rhythms to those of speech. Of this technical aspect of Miss Riding's poetry I shall speak later.

Miss Riding's limitations as a philosopher are clearly revealed in her "Disclaimer of the Person," which is tediously repetitive. Not satisfied with "cogito, ergo sum," she plays boundless variations on the theme. Her positive qualities are evident in many poems of genuine poetic quality. She has a strong sense of the necessity for oneness for a happy life. Even the slightest activity —say the achievement of a simple thing, even a word—involves an essential multiplicity of ideas. To achieve a complete life is a far more difficult task; but however short, it is adequate because it brings us nearer to unity or God. This unity, however, as I understand her, cannot be completely achieved until after death. Man does desire to share companionship, but the integration of self is the desired end. Or, to quote:

> *One self, one manyness*
> *Is first confusion, then simplicity.*
> —"One self."

It is only as we can lose all sense of self that we can become One, just as it is true that until we can see the many beauties as One we have not reached the desired goal. Pain can help us to this wholeness, but it is only an inch and not a secure inch.[1]

It is only natural that with this constant desire for "wholeness" the poet should be deeply concerned with the nature of reality, the meaning of time, and with the nature of earth and immortality. Miss Riding is. She recognizes that reality is essentially a quality of the mind, and that mere physical sensations cannot constitute it. Her heaven is, in fact, not unlike Shaw's; it is the place where there can be no evasion of the

[1] "The Number," "Enough," "Hospitality to Words," "The Wind Suffers," "There is Much at Work," "Celebration of Failure."

105

truth. One must be willing to face danger, the interesting way of life. The poet's difficulty, however, is her pretentiousness, because she believes the only reality is that of the poet. This may, of course, be merely a problem in semantics, or of arguing in a circle. Anyone who apprehends the truth is a poet and the truth is that which is apprehended by a poet. But what is the truth? To Miss Riding it is an absolute and not as Mr. Hayakawa would have it—that which society agrees on. She more nearly approaches the solution to her problem, it seems to me, when she realizes that most persons fail of their goal in life because they do not persist in the act of becoming. It is this act of becoming that she so strongly and repeatedly stresses. One of the great difficulties with modern man has been his loss of a clear understanding of virtue and the rewards thereof. He has failed to be aware of the evil present and to find the goodness in it that, let us say, the poet can do.[1]

Miss Riding's treatment of time contains little that is unusual. We can recollect the past without desiring its recurrence, we can even obliterate it through an effort of will, we can grasp the present only as we see the past and future, and a moment that is not grasped is lost. ("A Previous Night," "Echoes" (11), "Ding-Donging"). She lifts the subject from the commonplace, however, by her treatment rather than by the profundity of her observations.

In her treatment of death, she can be wryly humorous or serious. "Chloe Or . . .," for example, treats it lightly. So, too, in a way, does "Room." "Death is the crumb," she says, to which all things come. Death, too, is a desideratum for the person afraid of life ("Back to the Mother Breast"). The poet feels, in general, that we pay too much attention to death and welcomes the signs that man is concentrating more on life here than on that after death. If a person has concentrated on the act of becoming, immortality is nothing but a continuance of this after

---

[1] "Echoes" (9), "Prisms," "Jewels and After," "Poet: A Lying World," "The Last Covenant," "Plighted to Shame," "A Need for Hell," "March, 1937."

the illness called death. ("Then Wherefore Death," "No More are Lovely Palaces," "Then Follows"). It seems to me that in "Then Follows" the lack of humility which I find in so much of Miss Riding's work manifests itself strongly. I feel a lack of the sense of pity which arises from the lack of contact with the soil. This may be one of the results of her expatriation. Rather closely allied to the foregoing poems is "The Signs of Knowledge," often deeply passionate in its statement, that the world will end when we lose our capacity to be aware of it. Unfortunately the poem is repetitious and too long for what she has to say. It is deficient in form.

It is natural to ask what is the poet's attitude toward the people she sees around her. She is not ambiguous in her statements. "The Quids" is an early indictment of the society of unthinking people. She continues her analysis in "Echoes" (10) in which she characterizes the average person as one who wishes everyone to be like him, but wishes the privilege to indulge himself in those things he denies to others. Some persons, of course, can never learn wisdom. Her more obvious statements occur in "Many Gentlemen," "The Need to Confide," "In Nineteen Twenty-Seven," and "No More Than Is," the last two containing her most powerful. Both strongly communicate the commonplaceness of unthinking man, but they go much farther. They pose the problem of the thinking persons in this society who comprise the minority. It is their tragedy, of course, because they alone are aware of the consequences of this commonplaceness.

As the result of a strenuous examination of the nature of herself, it is only reasonable that she should comprehend what is unintelligible to others. She makes a delightful preliminary statement in "Pride of Head": And it is from this place of pride that the poet attempts to understand herself—"the savage, half-awakened land" and to "civilize it." She is aware, however, that it is impossible to understand life unless one understands himself; but this understanding of self can only be achieved from contact with others. There is a mutual dependence, although there can never be complete understanding ("Advertisement," "The World and I"). She expresses the difficulty in the pessimistic "The Way It Is." I regret, however, that because Miss Riding has come to believe that "poetry . . . deterred rather than furthered the truthful use of words," quotation is impossible. Miss Riding realizes that in order to see oneself it is necessary to stand apart from oneself; and she does this admirably in the section "Sickness and Schooling" of "Memories of Mortalities." Here she gives us a clear and moving picture of her childhood. When she attempts, however, to become more abstractly philosophical, as she does in "Concerning Food," she becomes pompous. The robes of a sybil hang loosely from her shoulders.

One of the difficulties posed by her poetry is ellipsis—her demand on the part of the reader for the same, or even greater, agility in encompassing broad imaginative leaps; greater, in that what she seems to have encompassed in one leap was probably actually achieved by several. She has merely obliterated those markers. Manifestly, speaking of poems in one category does not preclude their being included elsewhere, and at no time should the reader think that I am attempting to give the complete poem. "John and I," for example, broadens her picture of the insignificant man; but it also does much more. An insignificant man can be significant to the poet if she fulfils herself by the expression of this insignificance. "Lying Spying" is similar in its effect, except here the poet has refrained from repeating the fulfilment she has derived from the experience. Because of this, it is a stronger poem. Miss Riding is, of course, fully aware of the power of imagination; she also realizes that truth is death to the imagination. Once a fact has been accomplished, however, the imagination is freed to build on that fact; and a poet, more than the ordinary person, has a capacity to react to abstract stimuli, a capacity which Mr. Bertrand Russell thinks to be one of the four important things we should educate for. Once we have conquered our fleshly desires, we should struggle for a communion of spirit with others. At such a time a devotion to philosophy becomes paramount. At such a time, too, emotion may be recollected in tranquillity and imagination *will* have removed the bitterness *from the actuality*.[1]

It is not my purpose to give an exhaustive exposition of all the subjects touched upon by the poet. There are many: nature ("So Slight," "Faith Upon the Waters"), silence ("Poem Only"), definitions ("Nearly," "As Many Questions As Answers"), free-will ("The Reason of Each"), purity of words ("Come, Words, Away"), and others. But it is important that we look briefly at her poems on love. Here we find her at her clearest and best. It is these poems that will largely determine her reputation, because it is here that she touches on the experiences which the reader can most readily share with her.

Her love poems, belonging as they do to all periods of her poetic life, reflect her changing attitudes. The early poems are more youthful in their simplicity. She is concerned with the recognition of love, with her awareness that there never is a pure and all-encompassing love everywhere at once, the anguish of separation and of physical longing, be it only the touch of a hand. She gives us a good picture of woman's love. It is not the worthiness of the beloved that counts, but the quality of the love given.[2]

A more unusual aspect of love is presented in "The Tiger," a poem of continuous struggle against passion until a sublimation is effected. I sense a feeling of frustration in this poem just as I do in "Is It Not Sad?" which gives it a sense of depth. It is in such poems, and particularly in such as "You or You," "Rhythms of Love," and "In Due Form," and not in her philosophical poems that Miss Riding is most successfully the poet. In "Rhythms of Love," for example, she not only achieves a sense of ecstasy but succeeds in explaining the unexplainable,

---

[1] "Chrysalis," "Helen's Burning," "Footfalling," "It Has Been Read By All," "After Smiling," "The Forgiven Past."
[2] "Several Love-Stories," "The Mask," "Take Hands," "To a Loveless Lover," "Druida."

and in "In Due Form" she expresses a universal feeling. Every person in love desires some means by which that love is made tangible and secure.

At times, Miss Riding seeks to minimize physical love. It is an effort of the head, however, rather than of the heart, because the passion is apparent, and shines forth in several other poems. What she says in "Letter to Man's Reasonable Soul," she seems to unsay in "Benedictory," in which she says by implication many things about love; in "Be Grave, Woman," where the movement of the verse reflects the passion; in "Wishing More Dear," and in "How Now We Talk," which confirm the fact that after the passion of love the participants reach a level of understanding hitherto denied them.

Such then, are some of the things about which she writes her poems. What are some of the devices by which she achieves her effects? Miss Riding has no use for rhyme and little use for rhythms with a definite pattern. Her "Americans" (1934), written in loose heroic couplets in an informal style, has little merit. Her observations are superficial and her humour heavy. It indicates an incompetence with one of the most common of traditional forms. It would be futile to attempt to scan her poetry in the attempt to find the means by which she achieves her poetic effects. Although she divides her poems into stanzas, and sets up her lines on a page in the manner of traditional poetry, I can see little basic reason for so doing. The rhythms are definitely prose rhythms, apparent in "Poet: A Lying Word." I can see little difference in effect whether a passage is set up as follows:

> *"I say, I say, I am, it is, such wall, such poet,*
> *such not lying, such not leading into. Await the sight,*
> *and look well through, know by such standing still*
> *that next comes none of you"*—(p. 235)

and

> *What to say when*
> *When who when the spider*

When life when space
The dying of oh pity
Poor how thorough dies
. . . . . .

(p. 87).

In neither case is it much more than nonsense. At such times she is too much under the influence of Gertrude Stein, the dedicatee of one of her volumes of poetry. She is more directly under her influence in the matter of involution. In her best work, however, whether in long or short lines, the suppleness of her rhythms controls the emotions of the reader and arouses in him a correspondence with the poet that is consummated in a sense of oneness.

Miss Riding only succeeds in confusing the reader (and hypnotizing herself) when she resorts to what for want of a better term I shall call her use of involution. At its most successful, it does convey a certain subtlety of nuance; at its worst, it is so much gibberish. The passage from "Footfalling," beginning "A modulation is that footfalling" might convey to some readers a certain indescribable activity, and in its context that from "Benedictory," beginning "You would see, and made a mystery to see" could for many readers add to the poem's significance. Such use of words, however, is the very essence of the short poem "Beyond." My personal feeling, however, from encountering it so frequently in her poetry is that it results from her failure as an artist first to apprehend what she is trying to communicate to the reader.

"Making a poem," she has written in *Four Unposted Letters to Catherine*, "is like being alive for always. . . ." It is only natural that in attempting to communicate what are essentially mystical states of being, she should make extensive use of figurative language, especially metaphor. This is her dominant figure although she makes occasional use of simile. Each dawn broke "unnoticed as a single raindrop," or the wind "springs like a toothless hound," or that incident which pained us to think of was "like a promise to oneself not kept." My impression is that she uses personification even more sparely. The poetic impulse (either metaphor or personification according to one's definition) is a "lyric crow smelling the near-corruption," and she speaks of the "negro centuries of sleep/And the thick lips compress/Compendiums of silence," or of the "dollish smile of people." The average people are "dressed skeletons" who "memorize their doings and lace the year/Into their shoes each morning." She speaks, too, of a person's "indoor face," the "pert grenades of summer," and "the thistle-patch of memory."

Most effective are her definitions. "True lavish," she says, "is the terrible;" "love but self-alienation!" "truth is anybody's argument/Who can use words untruthfully enough/To build eternity inside his own short mouth." She admirably catches the German character when she speaks of "punctilio and passion blending/To that slow national degree." "Grief," she says, is the "pang of democracy" and "our doomsday is a rabbit-age/Lost in the sleeve of expectation." In "The Talking World" she gives a good but lengthy definition of talk.

Miss Riding has a delicate and sensitive feeling for language and a supple and fluid sense of rhythms, often Biblical, that combine in her best work to give us poems of rare beauty.

I have said little of the poems that I believe to be unsuccessful. Apart from the poems that I am unable to read—and they are many—I think poems like "The Sad Boy," "The Lullaby," and "The Way of the Wind" are failures. There is a tendency on the part of the poet to think that anything that interests her, trivial though it be, is worth saying.

In their attitude toward tradition women are apt to be rather extreme. They either worship it too slavishly, or disregard it entirely. Miss Riding, like Miss Moore, is one of the latter. Since the music of her verse is like no one else's, although I occasionally detect a turn of phrase inspired by Hopkins or Blake, the reader must first familiarize himself with it before its beauty can be realized. Its beauty is most readily apparent in those poems which deal with the subject of love, experienced or sublimated, in which the experiences described are those closest to the realm of actuality. It is in these poems, and those dealing with the spiritual barrenness that the common reader will find Miss Riding at her best. It is these that repay the effort required by even the simplest of her poems.

[*Note:* It was not until I was collecting "permissions" for quotations in the present volume that I learned that Miss Riding has so changed her attitude toward her own poetry that she discourages any publicizing of it in any way. Her studies in the problems of language have altered her attitude toward poetry to the extent that she now believes that poetry deters rather than furthers the truthful use of words—and it was the truthful use of words that was her concern. Since, however, the present essay tends to support the idea that her practice did deter the use of words that she so strongly desires, I have chosen to let it stand.]

Robert Penn Warren

1905—

Mr. ROBERT PENN WARREN is the youngest of the poets associated with the *Fugitive*, one of the tenets of which was so-called Southern agrarianism. But nothing does so much harm to an original writer as to attempt to fit him into an -ism. Except for an occasional derivative rhythm from the dean of the group, Mr. Ransom, Mr. Warren differs from Mr. Tate as markedly as Mr. Tate differs from Mr. Ransom. It is true, of course, that the South provides the milieu for much of their work: their landscapes, their images, their characters and their environment, their incidents. Since they are Southerners that is to be expected. There, however, the similarity ends. It is obvious, I think, that the authors of three poems as different as "Antique Harvesters," "Ode to the Confederate Dead," and "The Ballad of Billie Potts," look at things differently. To do full justice to each we should forget they are, or were, part of a movement. After all, movement can be away from a centre as well as around it.

Mr. Warren looks at the Southern scene with a naturalistic rather than a nostalgic eye. He is aware of the general beauty and graciousness of some aspects of the landscape; he is equally aware of the hardness, cruelty, and deceptiveness of others. He has observed accurately and listened attentively to the cardinal, the jay, the buzzard; but he also knows the habitat and ways of the cottonmouth. He is aware of the declension in the people. He is content to give an accurate report of his observations rather than to recreate in his imagination a half- or non-existent past. These qualities are as apparent in his rhythms as in his subject matter. He makes extensive use, for example, of a long line

faintly reminiscent of that of Mr. Ransom, but with the graciousness squeezed out. Or so it seems on first reading. His line tends
to be hard and matter-of-fact. This is even truer of his shorter
line. His statement is clear, his images sharp and precise. He
will have no truck with cant and hypocrisy. His wit and humour
are brittle and incisive. The foregoing calls for elucidation.

"Pondy Woods" is an early, "The Ballad of Billie Potts," a
later essay of Mr. Warren in narrative poetry. The early poem is
the story of Jim Todd's attempt to escape after having killed a
man; the later is that of Billie Potts' unconscious murder of his
son. The mood of the first is enhanced by his depiction of the
buzzard in flight, by the movement of the water moccasin, the
detail of Jim's patent-leather shoes. It more nearly resembles a
traditional ballad in treatment, although the stanza is not the
traditional ballad stanza. In the later poem, the poet departs from
the strict objectivity of a ballad and intersperses throughout the
poem, but within parentheses, subjective material. Read without
this material we have a quickly moving story with the emphasis
on the main incidents, as in "Sir Patrick Spens" or "The Twa
Corbies," and not on the transitional and explanatory material
between those incidents. The material within the parentheses,
whether it be description of landscape, depiction of character,
suggestion to the reader to put himself in the position of the
characters, or generalizations, adds colour, depth, and suggestiveness to the narrative. The irregular lines, repetitions, earthy
diction and details enhance the effectiveness. The accuracy of
the poet's eye is evident in the landscape within the first parentheses.

> It is not hard to see the land, what it was.
> Low hills and oak. The fetid bottoms where
> The slough uncoiled and in the tangled cane,
> Where no sun comes, the muskrat's astute face
> Was lifted to the yammering jay; then dropped.
> Some cabin where the shag-bark stood and the
> Magnificent tulip-tree; both now are gone.

But the land is there, and as you top the rise,
Beyond you all the landscape steams and simmers
—The hills, now gutted, red, cane-brake and black-jack yet.
The oak leaf steams under the powerful sun.

An element of narrative underlies four poems which deal essentially with mental states. The effectiveness of these poems —"Terror," "Pursuit," "Original Sin: A Short Story," and "Crime"—depends to a great extent on the movement of the verse, as well, of course, as on the selection of details and on a diction that keeps the pitch low but intense. The following, from "Pursuit," is characteristic of the modulations Mr. Warren has wrought on the rhythms given a gracious cast by Mr. Ransom. His treatment of the caesurae heightens the ironic tone.

The doctor will take you now. He is burly and clean;
Listening, like lover or worshipper, bends at your heart;
But cannot make out just what it tries to impart;
So smiles; says you simply need a change of scene.
Of scene, of solace: therefore Florida,
Where Ponce de Leon clanked among the lilies,
Where white sails skit on blue and cavort like fillies,
And the shoulder gleams in the moonlit corridor.
A change of love: if love is a groping Godward, though
        blind,
No matter what crevice, cranny, chink, bright in dark,
       the pale tentacle find.

He flattens this line, even more in sections of his "Mexico is a Foreign Country: Five Studies in Naturalism." Nothing could better indicate the danger of pigeon-holing poets according to supposed critical principles than a comparison of this series of observations of an extremely perceptive eye with some of Mr. Tate's preciosities. Although not the most outstanding work of Mr. Warren, they reveal a concentration of earthy qualities that give his work solidity.

It would be a great injustice to him to neglect such poems as "Monologue at Midnight," "Bearded Oaks," "Picnic Remembered," "Resolution," and "Love's Parable." Here we find clarity mingled with deep feeling, a capability of passionate love, controlled by an analytical mind, and a potency of imagery that approaches metaphysical wit. There is graciousness, too, but it is a less overt graciousness than we find in a poet of Mr. Ransom's urbanity. The difference arises, I should say, as the result of a different earlier environment. I sense this difference of environment from the poetry of the two and not from any known biographical facts. Mr. Warren's background, for example, as it reveals itself in his poetry, contains a greater element of struggle.

One other group of poems calls for comment. These are short, concentrated, difficult when first read, and seemingly unrelated— "Ransom," "Aged Man Surveys the Past Time," "Toward Rationality," "To a Friend Parting," "Letter to a Friend," "Aubade for Hope," and others. Underlying these poems, however, is Mr. Warren's positive outlook on life. He may not be able to have Browning's easy optimism—as who can today?— but he does not despair. In "Ransom," for example, he recognizes that our courage may need "new definition," and he suggests that it might be achieved by love. But even when things seem bleakest, when the "fruitful grove, unfruited now by winter" offers no promise, even then

> Sweetly trifoliate strumpet spray of green
> And crocus-petal, pale, in secret are
> April's catalysis :
> —"Aged Man Surveys the Past Time."

This note of hope is not, however, for those who dwell in the past. Such "freeze downward." It is necessary to alter one's point of view, to seek new horizons. Or as he caustically remarks, they must "shuffle the picturecard mind and deal" ("Toward Rationality"). He bolsters this note of hope in "To a Friend Parting" and "Letter to a Friend," particularly in the latter. The catastrophic events of our age may have made "courage superfluous, hope a burden," but we must still live by them. Our unspiritual age may be "the time of toads' engendering," but we must face the future with courage.

It seems important that we should bear in mind the fact that one of the greatest signs of hope for us today is that even many who profess to see no hope lead lives of such sanity and decorum as to embody the hope they fail to see. Hope, says the poet in "Aubade for Hope," is "like a blockhead grandma [that] ever above the ash and spittle croaks and leans." Unrelated to the foregoing in subject matter, but important to a complete understanding of Mr. Warren are "Eidolon," an imaginative reconstruction of a hunt in the dark woods, and "Revelation," the effect on a sensitive boy of a mother's reaction after he had spoken harshly to her.

The more carefully one reads these poems, the more the effectiveness of the poet's images becomes impressive. Obviously, it is impossible to do more than suggest the treasure that the reader may seek for himself. Grief has a "smarting condiment," regret is "ambidextrous," fears are "old wranglers out of deep," and brothers are "stones on this moraine of time." We not only rest "upon the floor of light, and time," but as light withdraws, we are "twin atolls on a shelf of shade." His similes, too, are vivid and he makes more abundant use of alliteration than the reader is first aware of.

It is apparent from the foregoing that I think highly of Mr. Warren's poetry. There is a subtlety about it that is not readily apparent. I said earlier, for example, that his rhythms resembled those of Mr. Ransom with the graciousness squeezed out. That is not literally true. The oftener one reads the poems—not all of them to be sure—the more aware he becomes of a new music. There is graciousness in the rhythms, but they are less obvious. The reader who has not freed himself from a subservience to the music of the iambic foot will find some of his rhythms strange. He, however, who joys in the fact that English and American poetry is returning to the rhythms natural to English, before the leaden-eared nineteenth century critics uttered inanities about the dominance of the iambic line, particularly the iambic pentameter, will delight in the subtle music of Mr. Warren's verse. Mr. Warren possesses a delightful sense of humour, often a robust one, with a keen relish for the incongruous. There is a bantering tone to some of his work. This is a facet he more willingly reveals to the easy reader. To the reader, however, content to let his acquaintanceship ripen by easy stages, there is a warmth and charm that divert him from the more obvious work to that which requires careful attention. To derive the full flavour of Mr. Warren's achievement one should forget that he was ever part of a group; certainly he should not be linked with Mr. Allen Tate.

W. H. Auden: 1940 and After
1907—

I

SINCE Mr. Auden has taken residence in America he has published five volumes of poetry: *Another Time* (1940), *The Double Man* (1941), *For the Time Being* (1944), *The Age of Anxiety* (1947), and *Nones* (1951). These will provide the basis for the present essay, which from many points of view will supplement my earlier one in *Sowing the Spring* (1940). It will be readily apparent in the following pages that this is an instance of the child's being the father to the man. Although the same subjects reappear, the emphasis is different and the conclusions often contrary to the earlier ones. I said at the time that Mr. Auden was the "foremost of the younger group of poets"; the statement has more truth today. At his best, he is great in the thing said as well as in his way of saying it. Unfortunately, however, his greatness more often appears in his way of expressing himself rather than in the thing said. The catholicity of his reading, the suffering, pain, and disillusionment resulting from the failure of many of his political and personal hopes have given a depth and universality to his later work that were absent in his earlier. His constant experiments with vocabulary, diction, and rhythms give a musical felicity to his finest poems that place them among the best of contemporary works.

Mr. Auden has always been interested in the political scene; not the narrow one of partisan politics, but that concerned with the problem of man's relation to man. This interest is manifested occasionally in *Another Time*, dominates *The Double Man*, particularly the admirable "New Year Letter," occurs frequently in *The Age of Anxiety*, but is almost wholly absent from *Nones*. The treatment is sometimes ironic, but most often serious, even though the tone is never ponderous.

Aware in his earlier poetry of the breakdown of political and social institutions, Mr. Auden has come to a more mature understanding of the causes and scope of those "vast spiritual disorders," and he no longer sees any easy solution to them. The guilt lies everywhere and can only be cured by a dissemination of the truth of the causes. Man is frequently taught by pain, but, given a period of truce, he forgets his lesson. Unfortunately the majority of persons are unwilling to face the political realities and drug themselves lest they should see that they are frightened children "lost in a haunted wood." But it is impossible to avoid our political responsibility, because merely by being born, "we are conscripts to our age" and must do everything possible to alleviate conditions.[1]

No one can save himself by concerning himself solely with himself. No one exists alone, and "we must love one another or die." Although few grant this, some who are truly just, and who know, do exist, and it is these who must show us the "affirming flame."[2] A strongly ironic poem, "Refugee Blues," is an effective exemplum.

Mr. Auden has sought for the causes of the present *malaise*, and agrees with those historians who believe they stem from the Renaissance with the rise of the "empiric Economic Man." Of him it can be said that profit was "his rational incentive/And work his whole *exercitus*." In other words, ours is the end of the era that began with the Renaissance. This economic man would minimize the spiritual values. But even when he was at his strongest in the period of the Industrial Revolution, men like Blake, Rousseau, and others were sounding warnings which were not heeded, and not being heeded, led to his being captured by his liberty. More particularly, Mr. Auden points to the similarity

[1] "New Year Letter," ll. 236-293; *The Age of Anxiety*, p. 24; "September 1, 1939," stanza 5; "New Year Letter," ll. 1,162-1,177.
[2] "September 1, 1939," stanza 8.

of the ages of Marx and our own. Both were times of political upheaval. Marx was not, of course, the sole cause of what followed, but only one of many responsible for the end of an epoch.[1]

Such ideas are not, as I have suggested, unique with Mr. Auden, but are the results of his wide and catholic reading. A careful student of the era, he regrets that greater studies have not been made. From what has happened man has had a good lesson, but perhaps not a thorough enough one.

Man's dominance by the machine has, of course, necessitated a change in his pattern of life, since the local customs have been destroyed. In the country, men have a common goal; in the city, not. Here each can find the necessity he most desires, even if it be no more than to be a nobody ("The City"). The change wrought by the move from country to city is more subtly hinted at in "Gare du Midi." The machine age has, in reality, created a new barbarian:

> *factories bred him;*
> *Corporate companies, college towns*
> *Mothered his mind, and many journals*
> *Backed his belief.*
>
> —"Age of Anxiety," p. 24.

What the poet is really complaining of is, of course, the idea that man has lost his power to feel, whether it be toward one's fellows, or the world of nature, or the greater spiritual truths. It is this lack in our rulers that makes them so dangerous.[2] One of our difficulties today is that:

> *The last word on how we may live or die*
> *Rests today with such quiet*
> *Men, working too hard in rooms that are too big,*
> *Reducing to figures*
> *What is the matter, what is to be done.*
>
> —"The Managers."

[1] "New Year Letter," ll. 1,200-1,287; ll. 665-695.
[2] "New Year Letter," ll. 518-528; ll. 787-832.

So bad has the situation become that the most we can say is that "true democracy begins/With free confession of our sins."

Ours indeed, says Mr. Auden, is a tawdry age in which life has sunk to "one press-applauded public untruth" and we all march in step. Man, by insisting on too much security, has lost too much in other directions. He has a necessity for a sense of importance and constantly seeks ways to provide himself with this sense. What he needs above any of these things, however, is a share in a real republic of man where men meet to share their spiritual satisfactions. To achieve this real republic requires constant work. The average man cannot achieve it by himself. It is those aware of the truth who must nurse him to "sense and decency."

Mr. Auden is fully aware of modern thinking about the universe and would, I believe, agree that life has no inherent meaning except as we give it such. Much of the trouble today arises from a mistaken sense of values. The sea, for example, he says, can misuse nothing because it can value nothing. On the other hand, man overvalues everything,

> *Yet, when he learns the price is pegged to his valuation,*
> *Complains bitterly he is being ruined which, of course, he is.*
> —"For the Time Being," p. 6.

Certainly the characters in *The Age of Anxiety* do not take a romantic attitude toward life, unless we think of their attitude as a negative romanticism. It is no nearer the truth than is too rosy a picture. Life, for them, between the "white silence of antiseptics" connected with birth and death is "but a bubble between/And shame surely." The thing that will bring them to their spiritual home today—and it is the same as Herbert expressed in the seventeenth century—is "a sad unrest/Which no life can lack." Much of this unrest—we could call it loneliness—stems from the knowledge forced on many by the machine: that "aloneness is man's real condition." This, of course, is not an original thought with Mr. Auden. But as Prospero says to Ariel, "thanks to your service,/The lonely and unhappy are very much alive."[1]

Man's loneliness is the result of his too close absorption in his own ego, and the cure is to get that ego off centre. Actually, much of the present political mess, says Mr. Auden, is the self-consciousness of the ego.

> *That looks upon her liberty*
> *Not as a gift from life with which*
> *To serve, enlighten, and enrich*
> *The total creature that could use*
> *Her function of free-will to choose*
> *The actions that this world requires*
> *To educate its blind desires,*
> *But as the right to lead alone*
> *An attic life all on her own,*
> *Unhindered, unrebuked, unwatched,*
> *Self-known, self-praising, self-attached.*
> —"New Year Letter," ll. 1,401-11.

It is evident from Mr. Auden's treatment of love that its importance to him is as a means whereby man can regain the state of feeling of which the machine has tended to rob him. Love, of course, cannot be defined. In fact, he says in a popular song,

> *I've sought it since I was a child*
> *But haven't found it yet;*
> *I'm getting on for thirty-five . . .*
> —"Oh, Tell Me the Truth About Love."

It is, let us say, like this thing called "Law"; we all agree that it is, yet we can't define it ("Law, say the gardeners"). Love, he says, is a way of living and is possible between any things and persons as long as there is a mutual need. Worthiness in the parties is beside the point:

---

[1] *The Age of Anxiety*, pp. 44; 15; 27; "New Year Letter," 1,633 ff.

> *Lovers, like the dead,*
> *In their loves are equal;*
> *Sophomores and peasants,*
> *Poets and their critics*
> *Are the same in bed.*
> —"Sharp and Silent."

Were this an isolated statement, we could write it off as a bit of cleverness. But he repeats the idea more seriously in "New Year Letter" (518-527). It is only natural that holding these ideas his experience should have led him to think of the transitoriness of love ("As I walked out one evening"), and to apply that idea to what would happen to Ferdinand and Miranda (*For the Time Being*, p. 9). And how could his experiences lead him to think otherwise since he has been one of those persons who, to use Mr. Frost's terms, have been willing to "straddle." He is one of those who haunt bars lest they should see that they were

> *Lost in a haunted wood,*
> *Children afraid of the night*
> *Who have never been happy or good*
> —"September 1, 1939."

He has been at a "love-feast" as tawdry as it is possible to find in Greenwich Village ("The Love-Feast") and he suffered bitter disillusionment. Both "Chimeras" and "Secrets" express the natural outcome of such a way of life. It is often difficult to determine whether some of the poems are of a hetero- or homosexual character. "Not as the dream Napoleon" and "Where do They come from" seem to possess the latter character. It is not strange that Mr. Auden should have believed at one time, at least, that "existence is enough" ("Underneath the leaves of life").

The reader who can grasp the beauty of love in Mr. Frost's poetry can only regret that Mr. Auden has failed to find a similar beauty. He can readily understand that from an orderless personal life in which many of his experiences were possible, much suffering should result. There are indications, however, that he has altered his thinking on certain points. In *Another Time* he had recognized the difficulties of keeping his eye on the future:

> *It is so hard to dream posterity*
> *Or haunt a ruined cemetery*
> *And so much easier to be.*
> —"Hell is Neither Here Nor There."

Instead of existence being enough, however, he has grasped the greater reality (and he is much concerned with reality) that one should not confuse Being with Becoming, and that the important thing is to be steadily striving toward a greater becoming. This idea occurs at least twice in *The Double Man* and at least once in *For the Time Being*.[1]

Mr. Auden has also learned much about suffering. The Old Masters ("Musée des Beaux Arts"), he knew, understood the human position of suffering, but it was not until *For the Time Being* that he realized that his own attitude may have been wrong. "Can I learn to suffer," he asks,

> *Without saying something ironic or funny*
> *On suffering? I never suspected the way of truth*
> *Was a way of silence where affectionate chat*
> *Is but a robber's ambush and even good music*
> *In shocking taste.*
> —"For the Time Being," p. 11.

The reader may think that I am taking too many statements from the poems as phases of Mr. Auden's credo, whereas they are only the ideas of the characters in the poems. I think the poet himself comes to my assistance in his untraditional sonnet, "The

---

[1] "New Year Letter," ll. 341-350; *The Age of Anxiety*, p. 87; *For the Time Being*, p. 5; *The Age of Anxiety*, p. 54; "New Year Letter," ll. 65-66.

Novelist." The novelist must achieve empathy, the poet not. This indicates that when the poet uses dialogue, he uses it for the better exposition of his ideas, and not for a greater realization of character. There is a uniformity of style in *The Age of Anxiety* that would be inexcusable if he were trying to reveal character.

In his early poetry, Mr. Auden often gave us interesting autobiographic glimpses of his youth and young manhood. His work since 1940 adds to those glimpses, particularly those of the poet as artist. When he woke into his life, he says, he was not what he seemed: "beyond their busy backs [he] made a magic/To ride away from a father's imperfect justice." As we know from the early poems, his boyhood was spent climbing among abandoned mines, and those surroundings contributed "a mode of thought." His later work adds to the picture of the poet by revealing his concern with his craft. Whatever slovenliness Mr. Auden may permit himself as a man, he is aware of the necessity for order as an artist.[1] Where the dichotomy has been great, he believes the greater the honour due, particularly

> *If, weaker than some other men,*
> *You had the courage that survives*
> *Soiled, shabby, egotistic lives*
> —"New Year Letter," ll. 103-105.

The reader immediately thinks of Hart Crane. Mr. Auden is fully aware, however, that he has not always been true to himself as an artist. For, he says,

> *. . . I relapse into my crimes*
> *Time and again have slubbered through*
> *With slip and slapdash what I do.*
> *Adopted what I would disown,*
> *The preacher's loose immodest tone . . .*
> —"New Year Letter," ll. 218-222.

[1] "New Year Letter," ll. 898-974; 1,686 ff.; *For the Time Being*, p. 14.

Later, he realized that when he was not in the mood to write, it was better not to try ("Cattivo Tempo"). He is sceptical, too, of the *vates sacer* concept of the poet. What the poet does is to rummage into his living and to fetch out the images "that hurt and connect" ("The Composer"); and, by painstaking adaptation "from Life to Art" transmute those images into an artistic entity. Art cannot advise man because it presents "already lived experience." By making a synthesis of sense, feeling, and intelligence, art creates an order that helps develop our "local understanding." The establishment of this order in one's personal life constitutes the "state of the fulfilled." Every sincere artist continuously doubts his worthiness. He is not so concerned with common approval as he is with the idea that he would like to think that he had the approval of certain artists of the past. In Mr. Auden's case, it is the approval of artists like Dante, Blake, Rimbaud, Dryden, and others.[1]

Many of Mr. Auden's best poems since 1940 are occasional poems such as his "In Memory of W. B. Yeats (d. Jan. 1939)," "September 1, 1939," "In Memory of Sigmund Freud (d. Sept. 1939)," "Under Which Lyre," and others and cover all emotional moods. The first two, especially, rank with the greatest modern poems. They are superb examples of the poet's art.

II

If the changes in Mr. Auden's treatment of his subject matter are only those resulting from maturity, the same may, I think, be said of the changes in his technique; one of the most apparent being the steady tendency to lighten his rhythms and give them a greater flexibility. Those in *Another Time* are slower paced and less subtle than those in *For the Time Being* and *Nones*. But generalizations are apt to be misleading. Let us con-

---

[1] "New Year Letter," ll. 52-98; 127 ff.

sider, therefore, a few specific examples. In "Wrapped in a yielding air," the rhythms are quite regularly iambic, and the attractiveness of the stanzas lies not so much in the delicately modulated music of the lines, as in the clever use of repetition. Here is stanza 2:

> *Beneath the hot incurious sun*
> *Past stronger beasts and fairer*
> *He picks his way, a living gun*
> *With gun and lens and bible,*
> *A militant enquirer,*
> *The friend, the rash, the enemy,*
> *The essayist, the able,*
> *Able at times to cry.*

The idea of repeating words like "gun" in lines 3 and 4 and "able" in lines 7 and 8 is found in every stanza, but never in exactly the same way. The slight variations keep the reader alert. But within the movement of the line there are no unconventionalities. An early example of a more subtle internal movement is found in "The Capital," of which the fourth stanza has perhaps the greatest subtlety. The traditional notation breaks down and a musical notation gives a more satisfactory idea of the music of the stanzas.

But the sky you il-lu-mine, your glow is vis-ible far

In-to the dark coun-try-side, the e-nor-mous, the fro-zen,

Where, hin-ting at the for-bid-den like a wi-cked uncle,

Night af-ter night to the far-mer's chil-dren you be-ckon

In "New Year Letter," Mr. Auden avoids the danger of prolixity inherent in octosyllabic couplets and succeeds in adjusting thought to tone in such a way as to enhance the effectiveness of his communication. The flexibility of his couplets is that of a master and his medium fits his multi-purpose: reasoning, description, autobiographic reminiscence, and so forth. Some readers may be inclined to object to the many foreign words which he uses with blithe insouciance—Latin, Greek, Italian, French, and German—but he handles them with such an easy grace that it is difficult to object to them.

Freer rhythms appear in parts of "The Quest" where one can detect, I believe, the influence of Ogden Nash. Such rhythms are admirably suited for humorous and satiric verse, and that is the way he uses them in "The Way":

Forgetting his in-for-ma-tion comes most-ly from mar-ried men

Who liked fishing and a flut-ter on the hor-ses now and then.

The rhythms in *For the Time Being*, although lighter than those in *Another Time* and *The Double Man*, remain essentially traditional. This lightness is also apparent in *The Age of Anxiety*, but his over-use of alliteration becomes fatiguing and dissipates rather than concentrates the thought. The verse conveys the sense of a lack of contact with the earth. It remains too cerebral, yet it is not closely knit.

Mr. Auden's more radical innovations in rhythm appear in his latest volume *Nones*. They reveal the influence of some of our older poets of the *avant garde*. The unrhymed lines of "In Praise of Limestone," for example, often strongly monosyllabic, possess a movement quite different from anything he has previously written:

Watch, then the band of ri-vals as they climb up and down
Their steep stone gen-nels in twos and threes, some-times
Arm in arm, but never, thank God, in step, or en-gaged
On the sha-dy side of a square at mid-day in
Vol-u-ble dis-course, know-ing each o-ther too well to think
There are a-ny im-por-tant se-crets. . . .

In "Their Lonely Betters," the music is strongly reminiscent of Mr. Frost, but in the unrhymed "Air Port" the music is distinctive, modern, and typically that of Mr. Auden.

In *Another Time*, similes are rife, and often give us an insight into the poet. The conspiracies of children are, for example, "weak like the vows of drunkards" (8). The rooks in the garden "like agile babies still speak the language of feeling" (9). Housman kept his "tears like dirty postcards in a drawer" (11). And of Edward Lear, "children swarmed to him like settlers. He became a land" (12). The rebel angel "like influenza . . . walks abroad" (13). The poet is "encased in talent like a uniform" (33). The full moon high over France is "cold and exciting/Like one of those dangerous flatterers one meets and loves/When one is very unhappy" (47). It would be easy to increase the number. In his later volumes, however, similes occur more rarely and metaphors and incisive epithets take their place.

I have mentioned Mr. Auden's predilection for alliteration in *The Age of Anxiety*. Alliteration occurs frequently in all of the volumes, and is closely connected with his experiments in diction, experiments which have assumed much greater importance in the later volumes than in the earlier. In *Another Time*, for example, I noted only seven words that might be unfamiliar to the educated general reader and even many of these could easily be guessed at from the context. In *The Double Man*, thirteen; in *For the Time Being*, six; in *The Age of Anxiety*, thirty-nine; in *Nones*, thirty. A further breakdown of these words shows that twenty-four are printed in pearl type at the bottom of the pages of *Webster's* unabridged dictionary and are listed as Scottish or English dialect or rare; not listed either in Webster or the Shorter Oxford are fourteen; twenty-four are not commonly used although they are listed in regular type.[1]

It is evident from the poet's use of these unusual words that no easy generalization is possible, except, perhaps, to say, crudely paraphrasing one of the poems in *Another Time*, that he has walked through the dictionary hoping that by chance some of these words would come true. Let us generalize on the basis of the words in pearl type, considering first those he uses with greatest effectiveness.

Psychopompos: a guider of souls. This is necessary for the rhythm.

> *The candid psychopompos spoke*
> —"The Double Man," 24.

Widdershins: (variant of withershins): in a direction contrary

---

[1] The number of words in the first three volumes is relatively small compared with the last two. We find in the former: *matrilineal, psychopompos, widdershins,* and *louche.* But in the last two we have *ascesis, Mimas, watchet, pursive, relievos, abrupt* (as a verb), *hepatoscopists, catadoup, chafant, fabbling, siblings, dedolant, baltering, sossing, qualming* (verb), *mornes, motted, mamelons, sottering, frescade.* Not listed are *fragible, vorpal, cryptozoon, deisal, oddling, pyknics, perameters, gennel, cerebrotonic, soodling, megalopods, mesomorph, hideola, prosopon* and others. Some of these have, of course, come into use more recently. Among the other words that are not commonly used are *catabasis, centrosome, discrete, freemartin, wabbles, morphon, tourbillion, sophrosyne, tundras, fioritura, seizin, esker, volant, wyvern, dotterel, dunlin, fucoid, wambles, dædal, cabaletta, pinguid, lustrate, jussive, indagation,* and others.

132

to the apparent course of the sun. By its use Auden achieves
a nice concentration in the couplet:

> *A witch self-tortured as she spins*
> *Her whole devotion widdershins.*
>
> —"The Double Man," 62.

We must face the fact, however, that perhaps the witches
were introduced because of *widdershins* and not the word
because of their actions, essentially symbolic.

Ascesis = asceticism. This is necessary for metrical uniformity.

> *Ascesis of their senses*
>
> —"For the Time Being," 90.

Dedolant: feeling no grief or compunction. This is an accurate use of the word to heighten the emotive quality of
the poem.

> *A tanker sinks in the dedolant sea*
>
> —"Nones," 39.

Baltering: dancing or treading clumsily. This creates an effective image.

> *. . . the baltering torrent*
> *Shrunk to a soodling thread.*
>
> —"Nones," 45.

Frescade: a cool bower. This sharpens the image.

> *A commuter's wish, where each frescade rings*
> *With melodious booing and hooing.*
>
> —"Nones," 72.

In many instances, however, Mr. Auden sacrifices sense or
clarity for sound or cleverness. The following words are used
loosely and inaccurately.

Sossing: plunging or thumping. Is this meaning in accord
with the rest of the passage?

> *The three wise Maries come*
> *Sossing through seamless waters, piloted in*
> *By sea-horse and fluent dolphin.*
>
> —"Nones," 45.

Faffling: stammering, stumbling. This is inaccurately used in
> *Horseback under his faffling flag*
>> —"Nones," 25.

How does a flag stammer or stumble?
Louche = slouch. This word does not make sense in
> *Pursue a louche and fatuous fire*
In French *louche* means equivocal, but an equivocal fire is
little better.
In the following, alliteration determines the poet's choice:
Sottering: boiling. The word sharpens the image.
> *The sharp streams and sottering springs of*
> *A commuter's wish . . .*
>> —"Nones," 72.

Pursive: short-breathed, asthmatic.
> *Parapet of some pursive fountain*
>> —"The Age of Anxiety," 81.

Isn't the association unfortunate, even though accurate?
Relievos: reliefs. Inaccurate image.
> *From lawns and relievos the leisure*
>> —"The Age of Anxiety," 72.

Watchet: wet-shod. Redundant.
> *. . . where bathers basked beside*
> *The watchet waves*
>> —"The Age of Anxiety," 37.

Hepatoscopists: divination by inspecting the liver of animals.
Good satiric effect.
> *But peace was promised by the hepatoscopists*
> *As the ministers met to remodel the Commonwealth*
>> —"The Age of Anxiety," 121.

The next three words taken together are redundant. The picture
is confused, but the words approach pure music with their
alliteration and subtle vowel gradation.
> *Mornes:*   a rounded hill
> *Motted:*   a clump of trees on a prairie

Mamelons: a rounded hillock
> *Mornes of motted mamelons*
> > —"Nones," 72.

At times, however, Mr. Auden uses a strange word when a familiar one would be almost equally effective, and would certainly make a more accurate communication with the reader.

Catadoup: a cataract (obsolete).
> *The forthright catadoup*
> *Shouts at the stone-deaf stone*
> > —"Nones," 19.

Chafant: enraged.
> *Chafant or outwardly calm*
> > —"Nones," 19.

Occasionally, however, it is a question of accuracy or of evocative quality. For example, in the line "*Dotterels* and *dunlins* on its dark shores" (*The Age of Anxiety*, 59), there are many beauties and although less vivid to the general reader than "Plovers and sandpipers on its dark shores" the use of the less familiar words is justified.

"Oddling" in "oddling angler" is undoubtedly one of the poet's own coinages and the meaning in its context is readily apparent. He frequently uses familiar words in a strange way; for example "tacit tarn." "Tacit" does mean quiet, of course, but not in the sense of describing a quiet mountain lake. The choice is obviously for the sake of alliteration. It is apparent, I think, that often he strains too far after cleverness. He is brilliant and talented enough to resist these egotistic impulses. The notebooks support the foregoing statements. Scattered throughout them are lists of words arranged alphabetically.

Mr. Auden is not, nor will he ever become, an American poet in the way that Mr. Frost, Mr. Williams, or Mr. Ransom are American poets, and he is fully aware of the fact. In his last two volumes, however, the American scene plays a more important role than in his earlier. In his landscapes the English countryside is his model; in his city scenes it is New York. Although Mr. Auden's poetry occasionally touches the heart, his appeal is essentially to the mind. Even the beauty of his finest rhythms seems divorced from the earth in a way that is never the case with Mr. Frost or Mr. Williams. They convey the sense that this inspiration has been largely a literary one.

Mr. Auden frequently achieves a curious juxtaposition of styles in one work. This is more apparent in *For the Time Being* than elsewhere, but it is not confined to this Christmas Oratorio. It occurs in isolated lines like "red flannel *scivvies* for heroic *herms*," but most frequently in his lighter verse where it provokes laughter in the reader. And Mr. Auden's light verse is the finest that we have today. His rapier-like wit, his deftness with his rhythms, his command of the right word combine to give us poems that are unequalled of their kind. When a serious subject deeply moves him, his superb technical equipment enables him to do it full justice. He is capable of deep feeling and he occasionally permits us to glimpse it. On the whole, however, he presents a harder surface to the world, and the moments when he reaches the heights have become less frequent. Although it is to be regretted, it is not to be wondered at. The careful reader need not know more than Mr. Auden has told him in the last five volumes to understand the reason.

ACKNOWLEDGMENTS

Brandt and Brandt: "The Jig of Forslin," "The House of Dust," "Preludes for Memnon," "Music I Heard With You," from *Collected Poems of Conrad Aiken*, published by Oxford University Press, copyright 1916, 1920, 1930, 1931, 1953, by Conrad Aiken.

Committee for Ezra Pound: See under New Directions.

Eyre and Spottiswoode: See under Alfred Knopf, Inc., and The Macmillan Company.

Faber and Faber: See under The Macmillan Company and Random House, Inc.

Harcourt, Brace and Co., Inc.: "The Ballad of Billie Potts," "Pursuit," "Aged Man Surveys the Past Time," from *Selected Poems: 1923-1943*, by Robert Penn Warren, copyright 1944, by Harcourt, Brace and Company.

Henry Holt and Co., Inc.: "Former Barn Lot," "All of the Steps," "Night's End," from *Collected Poems: 1922-1938 of Mark Van Doren*, copyright 1939, by Mark Van Doren.

A. M. Heath and Co., Ltd. (through the courtesy of Nannine Joseph): British permission for the three foregoing poems by Mark Van Doren.

Alfred Knopf, Inc., and Eyre and Spottiswoode: "Winter Remembered," "Necrological," "Janet Waking," "Dead Boy," "Antique Harvesters," from *Selected Poems of John Crowe Ransom*, copyright 1945, by Alfred Knopf, Inc.

Alfred Knopf, Inc.: "Elegy: On a Dead Mermaid Washed Ashore at Plymouth Rock," "XXth Century," "Lost Twilight," " A Soft November Night," "Reflections on Still Water," "Andante Simplice," "The Demigod," from *Poems for Music: 1917-1947*, by Robert Hillyer, copyright 1947, by Robert Hillyer.

"Let No Charitable Hope," "Viennese Waltz," "Little

137